GETTING
OFF THE
PORCH

MY JOURNEY TO LIVING A FULL AND AUTHENTIC LIFE

GETTING
OFF THE
PORCH

MY JOURNEY TO LIVING A FULL AND AUTHENTIC LIFE

ALICIA BOOKER

Published by Mynd Matters Publishing
201 17th Street NW
Suite 300,
Atlanta, GA 30363
www.myndmatterspublishing.com

Identifiers:
Library of Congress Control Number: 2017917483
ISBN-13: 978-0-9981990-9-2 (pbk)
ISBN-13: 978-1-948145-99-2 (hdbk)
ISBN-13: 978-1-948145-00-8 (ebook)

FIRST EDITION

For my children,
Amber, Jordan, and Kendall,
You are my why.

Love,
Mommy

CONTENTS

FOREWORD

*T*he story you tell about your life, and even more importantly—how you tell it, gives a glimpse into your spirit. To tell your story well, you must embrace not only the beautiful, happy, and proud moments, but also the heartbreaking, regretful and uncomfortable ones. To do so is to own your story. And that is exactly what Alicia Booker does in *Getting Off the Porch.*

Owning your story is a brave act. It is to accept your life as is, and make a decision to make the most of it. It is to examine all that you have experienced along your journey and glean wisdom from it. It is to embrace the most heart-wrenching pieces and say, "I will be better and not bitter." Owning your story frees you to step outside of yourself and recognize your role in writing it. Whatever your story to this point, the rest is still unwritten.

I met Alicia several years ago as she was taking her initial steps "off the porch." I didn't know what she was going through at the time, but I knew she'd discovered a sense of purpose similar to my own—using the power of coaching and communication to inspire others to live more fulfilling lives. She was a student in my coach training program at the Coaching and Positive Psychology (CaPP) Institute. Like so many students from around the world who've been through the program, she was excited and passionate about personal and spiritual growth. She continued on to our Certified Personal and Executive Coach program, and was one of the top graduates in her class.

It was around that time that she reached out to our office to ask if she could volunteer at our next training since she lives in the Atlanta area where we are located. For three days, she enthusiastically served, smiled, and shared with students how coaching had helped her break out of the box and see inspiring opportunities for her future. Our students, who could relate well to her authenticity and passion, followed her lead. Many of them went on to become Certified Personal and Executive Coaches because of Alicia's testimony.

Little did I know at the time, she lives just minutes from me and my family. Today, she is not only a facilitator in our program, but my personal friend. We have spent hours talking about her story, her book, her leap of faith out of the corporate world and into the world of solo entrepreneurship as a life coach and an author.

She never stopped sharing her vision and boldly taking steps towards it. I am proud of her. Perhaps, in part, because I relate. I've been there. In 1999, I made a similar leap—writing my first book and publishing it myself, hopeful it would resonate. Now writing my twelfth book, I know this work of personal growth takes relentlessness and belief, discipline, passion and a lot of perseverance.

I am thrilled that she has the courage to not only own her story, but to share it with the world. It is one thing to reflect on your life in the privacy of a conversation with your closest confidant or the pages of your personal journal. It is another entirely to share with those you don't even know, in hopes that it might resonate and inspire them.

We often think our journey is all about us. But ultimately, it is about others. When you are willing to be transparent enough to tell your truth, your story, you open the door to inspire others with theirs. As she told me during her writing process, "It is scary to put my story out there, but it is also freeing. Even more than that, to have my children know my truth and my story means I am modeling for them what it means to be brave. That is a legacy I am proud to create."

At the core of my message is getting the courage to live the fulfilling life God has for you. Getting unstuck always begins with telling yourself the truth. The truth about your life, your relationships, and about the hopes and dreams that have been divinely placed in your heart. I hope from Alicia's story, you are moved to intentionally write the forthcoming chapters of your own life and to get off the porch and step out of your comfort zone, to live life wholeheartedly and have hope, especially when you are uncertain of what the future will hold. If you are willing to do the work of personal and spiritual growth, I believe the best is yet to come.

Be brave,

Valorie Burton

Author, *Successful Women Think Differently* and *Brave Enough to Succeed*

INTRODUCTION

*T*his book has taken me more than three years to write. Mostly because it was written as my journey took shape—in real-time. In the not-so-distant past, I had the perfect life: a successful husband, beautiful home, nice cars, three beautiful children, and even the world's best dog. Then, life happened. The following pages are filled with my journey through that unpredictable reality. Because my marriage comprised twenty years of my adult life, it is a big part of the book's content. However, *Getting Off the Porch* is not about my marriage. It is about finding myself within the confines of the "perfect" life I created.

When I married my knight in shining armor, we were both what the other needed. We were a team, and even though our journey has taken us through some really dark places, my heart was pure throughout. Although our marriage didn't survive, I do not regret one day of it. I am forever grateful for the family we created together. We didn't know it at the time, but we were broken when we met and the wounds of our past are what ultimately ended our partnership. We will always be family, and prayerfully, this book will continue to heal us, ushering in a new chapter filled with authentic joy and peace. By no means am I an advocate for or against divorce. I am an advocate for living authentically and owning the power of your story. So many of us live in shame or fear, and try to suppress the very story that shaped us into who we are, whether we like that person or not. My hope is that by telling and owning my story, it will help you dig deep to find the courage to live your truth no matter where the path may lead.

The greatest motivation for writing this book was my children. I discovered my worth and value on my *Getting Off the Porch* journey, but it was my desire to be better for them that got me through my toughest days. I want to break the cycle of unworthiness and playing it small. I want them to know that I am not perfect, and no longer require perfection from them. I want them to know that they are enough, period. I could not teach those powerful lessons until I believed and lived them for myself.

Getting Off the Porch represents the amazing journey that is life. It was written to empower and inspire you to find and live your truth. By sharing my life in all of its imperfection, I hope you will have the courage to own your story and embrace the power that comes from gaining authentic clarity.

The following chapters capture the many rich relationships I have been blessed to have, along with my growth, my falls, my choices (positive and negative), and all of my imperfections. I hope my journey off the porch will inspire you to be brave, face your greatest fears, and find the strength to get off the porch yourself!

PART ONE

FACING MY FEARS

CHAPTER 1

PICTURE PERFECT

"You can't be brave if you've only had wonderful things happen to you."
-Mary Tyler Moore

At approximately 7:59pm on October 6, 2011, was the last time I remember thinking I was happy in my life. In my eyes, my life was picture perfect: a successful husband, a job I loved, three beautiful kids, a beautiful home, a nice car, and even the perfect dog. My life was more than I ever dreamed it could be, and you would not have convinced me otherwise. Sure, there were times when I felt *something* was missing. Times when I was searching for something, but had no idea what. Times when it was clear that perhaps there was a side of my husband that was disconnected and dark. But even in those rare occasions when I allowed my mind to wander from being perfectly content with my life, I was still happy, because didn't I have it all? I worked hard to create a life that was far from the family life I had as a child, and I had to fight to protect that. Didn't I?

It was my husband's birthday, and this day started like any other. I woke up and got the kids off to school, got myself ready for work, kissed my husband goodbye, and wished him a happy birthday. I stopped by the market on my way home from work to prepare his favorite meal for dinner and pick up a birthday cake. It was a great night with lots of laughter and chatter. We had our usual birthday dinner and cake to celebrate him on his special day. The mood was light and we were all enjoying being together, cleaning the kitchen, being silly, dancing, and all of the normal evening banter. As I was loading the dishwasher, I noticed his cell phone on the counter. I picked it up and started to read aloud all of his birthday texts. The kids and I were excited to see certain names, and it always amazed me that so many people wanted to wish him a happy birthday. As I continued reading, I came across a text message from a woman I did not recognize, and the content was very sexual and inappropriate. I caught myself before reading it aloud. I told the kids, "That's enough for now. Let's get this kitchen cleaned up." While my children did not notice the change in my facial expression, I am sure my sudden change made my husband very uneasy. I gathered myself and finished the evening routine without a hitch externally. Internally, it was as if I had been punched in the gut and the air was leaving my lungs. Everything was off-kilter, and my body was uneasy. I felt flushed and stunned. It took everything in me to remain calm in front of the kids.

After the kids were in bed, lunches were packed, and the kitchen was cleaned, he stood in the kitchen looking through mail. I walked over to him, and an unfamiliar version of myself emerged. I picked up his cell phone and threw it on the counter.

"What the fuck is this?"

I had never cursed at him before, but lost control of being the sweet, perfect Alicia. I got the "what are you talking about" expression, but he soon realized exactly what I was talking about. I went on a rant about the actual exchange, and started asking specific questions. This woman wished him a happy birthday, but it was he who initiated the sexual conversation. Who is this woman? Why are you speaking to her this way? Have you been with this woman? Are there more women that you communicate with like this? The list went on and on and I pushed for answers. He gave a pretty lame explanation.

"It's nothing. Just something to do. It means nothing. Nothing ever happened. It's just talk."

I would have probably accepted all of those ill-conceived explanations had I been able to breathe. But the sinking feeling in my gut was so huge that this time, the explanation wasn't enough. I interrogated him more. I wanted to know every detail. I wanted to know how this could have happened. How long it had been happening? How many women was he sexting? I wanted to know it all, but after hearing the details that he was willing to share, it did not make a difference. In that moment, the picture I believed in, the picture I put every ounce of my being in, was shattered.

That night, I could not and did not sleep in our bedroom. My youngest child always got up and came to our room, so when she came to get into my bed, I went and slept in hers. My heart was broken. I knew then that nothing would ever be the same, but I couldn't get past the heaviness in my heart to even see clearly.

I woke up early the next morning and did something completely out of character. While he was in the shower, I went on his cell phone, found the text, and responded to the woman. I told her how inappropriate it was to sext a married man and proceeded to lecture her about morals. After pushing send, I felt pathetic. This had nothing to do with her and everything to do with the fact that my marriage was not as sound as I had once believed. But in that moment, I couldn't face that truth. I was embarrassed and felt sorry for myself. Thoughts continued to plague my mind: How could he do this to me? I have been completely devoted to him for sixteen years. I did not deserve this! I was the victim and I filled the role, fully. For weeks, I opted not to share what had happened with anyone because I was so ashamed and embarrassed. We were the model couple and family. We were often told that others admired what we had. Instead of opening up, I walked around in a cloud of sadness and disappointment—and he let me. For almost three weeks, I drifted through life making sure my kids didn't sense anything was wrong, but lived with an internal sadness that was consuming me. I remember standing in my retreat, which is a large room off of my bedroom. A room designed for peace and tranquility. As I was ironing a pair of pants, my husband walked into the room. I stopped ironing and looked him squarely in the eyes.

"Are you going to just let me walk around here sad and desolate without any attempts to make this right?" He stood with a blank stare. In that moment, I realized he had done all he was going to do. He had apologized and was ready to move on. I was completely lost.

Several weeks passed and I could not move on. As we watched television one night, I told him that I could not get past it. I was trying but it was consuming me. Although he was trying to be understanding, he was exhausted by my inability to leave it in the past and move forward.

I asked him, "How would you feel if it was you who found the text messages?"

His response astounded me. "I would look within myself to see what might be missing or what I could do more of."

I was dumbfounded by his response, or shall I say, accusation. So now it was my fault that he was seeking attention outside of our marriage? It was my fault that he cheated on me? How dare he point the finger at me after all

I had done for this family. After all I had done to support him and his dreams. After all I had done to be there for him no matter what. I was no longer sad. I was mad! And I realized I needed to fight—fight for myself, not necessarily my marriage. I had no idea that this would be the best advice he ever gave me...

A Shift in Mindset

One night, while headed to my bedroom, I passed the television. Filling the screen was a famous civil rights icon with his wife by his side. Over the years, I had heard that this leader engaged in several extra-marital affairs, one of which was with my best friend's grandmother. I looked at the screen, and decided in that moment, *Hell No*! I will not be the dutiful wife standing by her man no matter what. My sentiment confirmed that I was still in the anger phase. Roughly a week later, I stood alone in my retreat as a feeling washed over me. I thought about that sweet little lady standing by her very accomplished husband. In an instant, I decided I would not be a victim and I would not be her. I would not give 150% of my heart and soul to this relationship, and only receive 85% back. His 85% included being a great provider, being there for our kids' sports activities, and helping around the house. However, the heart connection was not important to him. For years, I knew there was a piece of him I could not reach, touch, or penetrate. I wanted it, yearned for it, and fought for it, but it was unavailable to me.

With three young children, leaving seemed impossible, so I decided the only change I could make was in me. I returned to my role as wife without the sadness that had begun to overtake me, but my heart was different. Though the trust had evaporated, I tried to exist without dwelling on the text messages. Because being a wife also meant intimacy, I returned to our regular sex life. The first night I shared myself with him physically, I was emotionally disconnected. Or perhaps, it was no different than before, but this time I was the one who was different.

Once I decided to no longer be victim, I declared it to him.

"I've been thinking a lot about everything that has happened, and I realize I have to move forward." He seemed relieved.

I continued, "I've finally accepted that you have never been able to give me 100% of your heart, and that I will not fight for it anymore."

Sadly, he again seemed relieved. I went on to explain, however, that I will also not give 100% any longer. If all he could give was 85%, then that's all I would give.

Curious and a bit confused, he asked, "What does that mean?"

"I'm still figuring that out."

"Okay," he said before falling asleep.

Who goes to sleep after a statement like that? The simple act of him going to sleep with no further inquisition was the beginning of a realization about my marriage, about myself, and what I had accepted as normal for almost two decades and it terrified me. The chasm between us was more expansive than I had realized. Outside of the things that husbands do like provide and help around the house, he was unwilling or unable to do more. He did not listen. He did not see me. He did not communicate. Overwhelming sadness filled the void between us. Emotionally, I was receiving well below 85% which was unacceptable. My heart ached for more as I succumbed to sheer emptiness while listening to him snore fast asleep beside me.

For the first time in my life, I did not have a plan. I only knew that my life, and more importantly, I, was no longer the same. Each day unfolded with a new sense of awareness. I was open to the truth wherever it might lead. Prior to that night, my mind was closed to anything and everything outside of the world I'd created, but now I was navigating life differently. I did not know where it would lead; I definitely didn't think it would lead me to connect with another man. I definitely did not think I would get to know a part of me that I didn't realize still existed. I definitely did not think it would lead me to a place of peace, inner joy, and happiness. I definitely didn't think it would lead to the end of my marriage. I did not think any of those things because over the last 15+ years, I had not thought about myself. I only thought about my life as a unit, and I spent all of my time trying to keep it together by any means necessary. In doing so, I lost myself completely.

This was the beginning of a journey that made me look into the depths of my soul—into my fears and insecurities. I questioned everything I had once believed in.

CHAPTER 2
UNCONDITIONAL AWARENESS

"My love is unconditional. My trust and respect are not."

-Anonymous

*A*wareness is tricky. Early into my graduate studies in counseling, I learned the danger of awareness. Once you are aware, doing nothing becomes painful and uncomfortable. I was becoming more and more aware of "my stuff," and my desire to understand how I got here consumed me. As I began to get to know myself more, I decided that I would not be a victim. I had to figure out why I never required more. Why I overcompensated so much in the relationships of my life? Was I that insecure? Was I that afraid? I couldn't blame my husband, or my friends, or my family for my choices or actions. I knew the answers were in me. The questions just grew deeper.

Why did I look the other way, when I was taken for granted?
Why did I allow myself, my needs, and my emotions to be invisible?
Why was I such a rule follower?

Why was I afraid to ruffle the waters?
Why was I afraid to say no?
Why was I afraid of conflict in any form?
*Why was I afraid to disappoint everyone and
anyone?*
Why did I think perfection equaled love?

Questions flooded my mind and I began searching for answers. I gave myself permission to think and live outside of the safe, beautiful picture. The answers I needed were found in every piece of the limited 15% I had allowed myself to acknowledge and live within. Sadly, I don't believe my husband noticed a shift until it was far too late. At home, I was still a dedicated wife and mother. However, when I left home, I began to discover who I was outside of being the picture-perfect wife and mother. For years, the space beyond the confines of my home terrified me and had me living in fear. What would I find? How would I define myself? The fear was now replaced with curiosity and a desperate need to rediscover myself.

On the outside, life with my husband returned to normal, but my quest for understanding was ever present. No longer was I walking around sad and despondent. I was attempting to be present and not dwell on the sinking feeling in my heart that my marriage was in trouble.

One night, my husband, kids, and I watched the movie, *Unconditional.* It explored the power of love and connection. As amazing as I once thought my marriage and relationship was, I now questioned our connection. Although the love was still there, I felt miles away from the man that I once labeled my best friend. Our current dynamic felt like roommates sharing space. While my husband was physically and financially present, emotionally, there were huge limitations that I chose not to acknowledge. As a child, I yearned for security and for my dad to just show up, and I believe as an adult, I equated being present physically and being a responsible provider to love. Of course, I did not realize it at the time, but I was so desperate for someone to stick around and be there, that my emotional needs were secondary. After the movie, my husband was in the bathroom getting ready for bed. Clearly still emotionally overwhelmed, I sat on my side of the bed until he came in. The movie was about a couple deeply in love. The husband was brutally killed in a robbery, and it shows the wife's journey of recovery. It demonstrated how people, situations, and things are placed divinely in our paths to help us heal. At the end of the movie, the spiritual connection between the husband and the wife was so deep. It made the lack of connection with my husband appear enormous. I looked up at him and told him how I was feeling. As tears fell from my eyes, I spoke.

"That is the type of connection I want for us. Before this man died, he held something in his hand that only she and he would know the meaning of, and in his last breath, he told the man that was sitting with him to give her a message."

My husband listened, and I believe he sincerely tried to get what I was saying, but the glazed look in his eyes spoke volumes. He wanted the conversation to end but out of obligation and husbandly duty, he stayed put. Maybe something was blocking him from seeing me or my profound desire to feel his heart. His eyes were saying, *here we go again*, but my heart was saying *how could we not go here when you haven't seen my heart, my soul, and all that is crying out to you*. In that moment, I realized that I had to figure out why. He had not changed, I had. I could no longer merely exist. Why had I allowed myself to fade into the background of our life...my life?

A Simple Request led to a Big Discovery

Around that same time, my younger brother was working on a documentary that involved him driving across the United States. While working on the project, he was away from his wife for long stretches of time. During the entirety of his time away, he had been writing a journal about her and to her and wanted to make it into a book as her Christmas gift. He asked if I would be willing to proofread it before it was finalized. Of course, I said yes. He sent over a few entries and after reading the first one, I was brought to tears. The tears were for a number of reasons. First, I was overwhelmingly happy that he had found his soulmate and his love for her was deep and unapologetic. Second, because it made the divide in my own marriage appear even wider. There was a time when his love for me was strong and unwavering, and he expressed it freely. In fact, early in our relationship, he wrote a book for me. When did we drift so far apart that neither of us recognized the distance until the gap seemed insurmountable? I discovered the answer over the next few years. The third reason I was brought to tears is simply because my heart yearned for that level of connection and no matter how hard I tried or pulled, I could not receive it and now had reached a point where I could not even give it. I told my brother not to edit any of the entries. They should be given to her in their rawest form. I am not sure if he listened, but I am positive that it was one of the best gifts his wife ever received. He gave her his heart in a bound book for Christmas.

CHAPTER 3
SITTING ON THE PORCH

"The first step off the porch is realizing how you got there in the first place."
-Alicia Booker

My Childhood Porch

*A*fter the movie and interaction with my brother, my journey to uncover the truth was accelerated. I went back, far back, to reflect on myself as a young girl on what could be considered my childhood porch. I ventured back to a time when my father, the first man I ever loved, broke my heart. The feelings of unworthiness in my marriage and during my childhood were similar. When I think about my father, a mixture of emotions come to mind. Until age ten, I could easily be defined as a "daddy's girl." It did not matter how much time, or even the quality of time I had with him, whatever he had to give was perfect for me. I loved my mother, but if my father was around, that's where I wanted to be. My love for him was pure...unconditional. He was cool, a musician, an artist, and he was mine. All of the kids in my neighborhood thought he was cool too, which also made me and my sister cool. As he walked down the street, people would raise their fists, say "what's up" and nod. He was bigger than life. School was roughly a mile and a half away from our house. As my sister and I approached the boulevard on our walk home, sounds from him playing the congas filled the air. Hearing the music made me happy because I knew it meant that he was home and he was happy. My father was both the epitome of fun and the best Kool-Aid maker around. I noticed the drunken stupors, his absence from the dinner table, the late nights, and the arguments, but none of that overpowered my unconditional love and commitment to him. He was my world.

Not long before my tenth birthday, my mother sat us down and explained that we were going to be moving into my grandmother's house (who had passed away earlier that year). My first question was, "What about Daddy?" When my mother replied, "Daddy isn't coming," my heart broke into a million pieces. I remember asking who was going to open the jars when they were closed too tight. I was trying to grasp on to something that might cause her to change her mind. Tears streamed down my face as I ran to my room and threw myself across the bed, crying for hours. I thought about my friends and the safety I felt in our small close-knit community. I grew up in a neighborhood with kids I had known my whole life, and we were all like family. We lived in a garden apartment community. We didn't have much, but I loved my life. My sister and I shared a room in our small, two-bedroom apartment. She hated sharing with me because I was a bit of a slob. However, I idolized my sister and sharing a room gave me a sense of security. I did not want my world to change, not a tiny bit.

After a short walk around the corner to my best friend's house, I shared with her what my mom had told me. Unfortunately, my sadness mattered little. My life, as I knew it, was changing and I had no say in the matter. My father (my world) was not coming with us and my life (as dysfunctional as it was) would never be the same. It was devastating to realize my lack of power. My vote didn't count, the adults in my life were calling all the shots, and I was not convinced that they knew what they were doing.

Fifth grade began with my recovery from a bout with pneumonia and a move to 235 Cleveland Street. Our house was large, old, and in a rougher neighborhood. The freedom and safety I'd felt in the garden apartments were forever gone and replaced with "do not go off of the porch." Drug dealers were common and the neighborhood kids much tougher. So, as a way of protection, my mother limited me to the porch.

My sister, my mom, and I were on this lonely journey to find some kind of normalcy in a place of sadness, anger, disappointment, resentment, and for me, withdrawal. I withdrew from my mom because she had changed my world without consulting me on what I wanted. My sister was angry and mean, and it seemed that my mere presence made her angrier and meaner. My mother was sad and lost. After all, she'd left my father and her mother and brother passed away all within a six-month span. I was consumed with my own pain; I never understood just how much she was drowning. Given her emotional state, she didn't have much left to offer her overwhelmingly despondent and lonely youngest daughter. She did what she could and though she may have wanted to give up on herself, I am forever grateful that she never gave up on me or us. Now that I am a bit older than she was at that time, my respect and admiration of her is infinite. I cannot imagine how she kept her head above water. She has since shared with me that it was us, her girls, that gave her the strength to keep swimming.

I withdrew from both my sister and mother and was more determined than ever to maintain the "fairytale" of my father and my importance in his life. Although I called him often, many times he did not return my calls. The longer I didn't hear from him, the more my heart hurt. The song, *Lately*, by Stevie Wonder was out at that time. I played it over and over again and wondered what happened to my dad. How could he not be missing me as much as my heart ached for him? I didn't understand what could be happening. About two weeks after we moved, I called. A woman answered and I quickly hung up the phone. I was astonished that someone else would be answering the phone. I could not imagine what could possibly be going on. I coped by making excuses for why he wouldn't call to check on us or simply to return my calls. I was confused. Being the youngest, my family would often leave out details as to protect me from things they thought would ultimately crush me. Their philosophy was, the longer they could shield me, the better. This was not the best strategy because usually, I had to figure things out on my own, and when I did, it was dreadful. What I soon learned was that my father had been having a relationship outside of our home for many years, and now had a new life with a woman, who was also having a baby. I didn't think I could get much sadder but what was left of my heart was crushed once again. The life I thought I had wasn't real and the father I adored, didn't have time for me anymore.

I still didn't give up. I wanted my daddy back and I needed to do whatever was necessary to get him back regardless of his amount of effort. There had to be some explanation as to why he kept making promises only to subsequently break them. Why would he agree to pick me up so I could ride on his bus (he was a school bus driver), and time after time, leave me waiting? He would literally just not show up. Each time we made plans, I never stopped hoping, waiting, or sitting on that porch, because he said he was coming. Hours would pass, yet, I never gave up on him. My mom would call me back inside, and I would get angry with her and my sister if they said even an inkling of a negative comment about him. I defended him endlessly and chose to believe the excuses he offered.

Reflecting on that time in my life filled my heart with pain and sorrow. I was blind to the impact that the many disappointments with my dad had on me. After watching that movie, it was like I was ten years old again. I felt inadequate, unworthy, and lonely. I could not get my younger self off of my mind. As I explored the pain, I realized that for most of my life, I'd been sitting on that porch waiting for someone to show up. Someone to tell me I'm enough and that I am worthy of love. Someone whose actions prove that I am important to them.

My dad was an alcoholic and drug abuser. Early in my life, I witnessed him being drunk and rolling marijuana joints. When I witnessed this at four-years-old, he told me he was making homemade cigarettes. When I announced to my mother that we would be rich because daddy makes his own cigarettes, it did not go over well. Before I was born, my dad battled with heroin addiction and got help through rehabilitation. However, though he stopped doing heroin, he battled alcoholism and smoking marijuana my entire childhood. Late in my teen years, it escalated again to cocaine and crack. I have no memory of a time when he was not addicted to some substance.

Growing up, my dad and I had a special connection. I always considered myself his favorite, not that it meant a whole lot, but deep down I believed he would show up, stop drinking, and stop doing drugs because I was special. That never happened and what I later realized was that I had decided on that porch that I was not enough for my dad to show up (in any way). I began (even at the age of ten) to lower my expectations and look outside of myself for anyone and everyone to save me from the loneliness of the porch and the constant reminders that I was not enough for him to love or be there for me.

I unconsciously put pressure on my husband to fill the voids and be everything my dad wasn't, even though that was not his job. Before we got married, we went to pre-marital counseling with our pastor. He asked us to communicate our deal breaker. I clearly stated that alcohol/drug addiction is my deal breaker. At that time, my husband didn't drink alcohol. That changed soon after we were married. He was by no means an alcoholic, but he would binge drink. Each time it happened, a piece of the security that he had once provided me slipped away. When he refused to acknowledge and understand why he repeatedly kept doing the one thing I'd said was my deal breaker, subconsciously, I felt the same way I had on the porch, and it terrified me. When my husband did not show up the way I needed him, I felt unworthy all over again.

Unfortunately, I didn't require more because I did not want to lose him or the security of the relationship. But most importantly, I didn't believe I was worthy of more.

About six months after my parents split, when my father continuously didn't show up, I realized that if I was going to have a relationship with him, I had to be part of his new family...so that was what I did. It was the start of my pattern of overcompensating. Over the next couple of years, I genuinely cared for his new wife and fell head over heals for my baby sister and subsequently, little brother. I looked forward to the time I would spend with them, because the loneliness in my own home was so vast that it was beginning to suffocate me. My sister and my mother were too consumed with their own pain and sadness to see me. I was lonely and lost and just wanted something to fill the gap. My new stepmother was closer to my age, spent lots of time with me, and the attention felt good. It wasn't from my dad, but it was something. I never took into consideration the effect that this closeness might have on my own mother. I was a child and finding a way to fill my own pain and loneliness was my priority. The more my stepmother filled the gap, the less I had to deal with my depressed mom and angry sister, and quite frankly, the less they had to deal with me. Whether her intentions were genuine or manipulative did not concern me at the time. It was not until years later, during my father's funeral, that I understood the level of deceit, manipulation, and pain that was inflicted on a little girl who desperately wanted love and acceptance at any cost.

Unfortunately, this period filled some major voids temporarily, but the things I witnessed would forever change the unrealistic fantasy I had created of my daddy and my new family.

I guess my new stepmother didn't really think through the decision to be with my father, because she married the same man that was broken and lost in addiction that my mother had. Though there were many problems between my mother and father, my mother did a hell of a great job protecting and shielding me from the worst of it. Now that I was cloaked in a new family dynamic and much older, that protection and shielding was gone. My stepmother treated me like her friend, and instead of protecting me, she shared everything with me and later, my older sister as well. From sixth grade through high school, I was exposed to everything from alcoholism, drug abuse, arguments, inappropriate settings, manipulation, just to name a few. I was unaware of the long-term effect it would have on me. With everything I was experiencing in my home life, I was still expected to go to school, do well, and grow into a normal teenager. Well, normal is relative. What I realized is that no matter how much I loved my father, I was not enough for him to do better, be better, and show up. As I developed into a young woman, I soon grasped that I would always feel a sense of inadequacy, because I made every wish, loved as hard as I knew how, prayed, and pleaded for my father to stop drinking, doing drugs, and get help. In the end, he not only lost his new wife and kids, but he lost the little girl that only saw the greatness in him.

The day I walked away was one of the saddest and scariest moments in my life. I was in college and had to go to his apartment for something. When I walked in, he was not there, but a group of young drug dealers were. I asked where my father was, and after they looked me up and down, they told me he had stepped out and would be back. A few minutes later, he came in, disheveled, and surprised to see me. A few of the drug dealers said, "This is your daughter? She's very pretty." He looked at them and then back at me and I saw a look of fear in his eyes, which was my signal to get the hell out of there. I hurriedly left but not before looking back at my father. My teary eyes met his and I knew I could never go back there again. In an instant, I learned I had no power over the drugs. I walked away that day and lost contact with my dad for many years as drugs began to destroy his life even further.

As I continued to reflect, it became clear to me that I'd depended on my closest relationships to save me from the isolation and disappointment I felt as a little girl on the porch. When those relationships let me down, or did not live up to my expectations, I found myself back on the porch waiting, or overcompensating for the disappointment as to not upset the other person. I could not bear the thought of someone leaving me. Even those that I should have let go of, I held on to. I did not believe that I alone was enough. My father's inability to choose me over drugs and alcohol along with his not showing up had solidified that I was not enough. In my mind, I resolved that if he really loved me, he would stop using drugs. If my husband really loved me, he would show up. If I was worthy, my father would stop drinking. If my husband cared about what mattered to me, he would not drink. My father wouldn't make promises he couldn't keep, because he knew how important trust was to me. In my marriage, my husband wouldn't lie because he cherished the fragility of my heart. Over and over again, I allowed this mindset to permeate my thoughts, interactions, relationships, and feelings. Because I didn't believe I was worthy, I did not require more, I tried my hardest not to disappoint, and I looked the other way. I had created a life full of safe and secure relationships and the more perfect I was, the better chance I had for people to stay. But this backfired in my marriage. The pressure I put on my husband to be perfect, made me oblivious to seeing him, his imperfections, or frustrations. Or when I saw them, I didn't create a safe space for him to own who he was. He lived in a space of trying to be who I wanted him to be and fighting against his authentic self. I told him I wanted to know all of him, but did I provide a space for him to be human? I am not so sure. This doesn't make up for the things he may have done or not done, but I have to own my part. My husband had his own issues, but what we developed over the decades was a paralyzing co-dependency that kept us stuck in complacency for fear of change.

Discovering this was both awesome and terrifying. Even though I desired so much more, getting off the porch was scary. It meant trusting and believing that I was enough. That being perfect was unattainable. That I had made some big mistakes along the way. That I had to start taking care of my own heart, even if it meant I had to do it alone. It meant that I would possibly have to face the fact that some of my "safe" relationships would possibly be shaken or even broken. I would have to change from the inside out. I would have to stop being an "enabler" and a "fixer," and instead allow others to step up to the plate. But what if they didn't? What would happen to me? Could I be okay with just me? I decided that I would never find peace or know for sure if my relationships, especially my marriage, were what I needed if I didn't require more. Again, I went back and reflected on who I once was, and searched for the light that once resided in my spirit. I knew my strength would come from that light.

CHAPTER 4
FINDING MY LIGHT

"There are two ways of spreading light: to be the candle or the mirror that reflects it"
-Edith Wharton

*M*y teen years were very tough, and I was a young girl trying to find her way. Though I've had so many aha moments now as an adult, during that time I was just trying to navigate life as best as I could with the situation I was given. I grew up in what many would call "the hood." I had to take two city buses to get to school, and during those long rides into the city, I developed a crush on the second person that would break my heart. I would just stare at him on the bus for like two years and imagine what talking to him would be like. We were in the same grade and class in middle school, but our interaction was limited until the ninth grade. I still remember it like it was yesterday. It was the early eighties, and I had on black jeans and an aqua shirt with my name in black going diagonally across the front of the shirt. This day, I felt particularly cute. The entire school took a picture in the gym, and as my girlfriend and I were walking back to class, he stopped me and talked to me. I tried my best to play it cool on the outside, while on the inside my heart was beating a million beats per minute. He asked for my number and I gave it to him, but then turned to my friend and was white as a ghost. I was panicked because he would be the first boy that would call me at home, and I didn't know how my mom would react. Yes, I was a freshman in high school, but I was a late bloomer. Hell, my home life was crazy, so who had time for boys. Well, he called and my mom didn't make too big of a deal about it. We talked, and he was everything I imagined he would be. We had an immediate connection, and I truly believe I loved him even before I ever spoke to him, but speaking to him just made it real. He connected with my soul from the first conversation. We talked about everything—his family, my family, his dreams, my dreams, and it was everything to me. We talked over the whole summer, and outside of my family, I felt like he had a window into my heart, and that terrified me. My heart was so fragile and already broken. When we went back to school, I began to avoid him because I was terrified of how much I cared about him. Talking on the phone was a lot different than seeing him and possibly being in a relationship with him. I just couldn't fathom being hurt, and the thought of a boyfriend scared me to the core, so I ran. This unfortunately has resonated in my life time and time again. I've had a tendency to run when scared or uncomfortable.

While I was running, he was a normal 15-year-old boy, and he found interest in someone else. By the time I realized this, and tried to run back to him, he had already gotten involved with her. I was so hurt, but yet I think I was a little relieved. I knew how deep my feelings were, and I knew how deep his were, so this other person gave us both the distance to yearn for what we had, but the excuse not to go for it. The next several years consisted of us trying to disconnect a connection that just wouldn't go away. The connection was deeper and stronger than either of us was ready for as teenagers, and in the process of figuring that out, he broke my heart several times, which led me to walk away for good. One day during those turbulent high school years, we were standing in the staircase of our high school and he said the following to me after I asked him, "Why do you love me?"

He answered, "You are the light amongst all this darkness that surrounds us."

I didn't completely understand what he meant then, but we both had a lot of darkness we were dealing with in our individual journeys. I knew I had a light. I knew I was very special and connected with people in a rare way, but at that time I also realized that my light was not enough. It wasn't enough for my dad, and it wasn't enough for my first love to fight for me. I let my light dim during that time, and it was replaced with insecurity and unworthiness. Because of the circumstances of my life, I convinced myself that I was not enough, and I stayed on the porch for 30+ years playing it safe, and being careful not to disappoint while overcompensating for everything I didn't think I was worthy of receiving.

During a recent run, the words, "you are the light amongst the darkness," came to my mind, and it made me smile. All those years ago he saw the light that shined so bright, but I allowed life's circumstances to let the flame dim, so low, I almost let it go out. I did have a light. A light that made me shine bright and spread and feel love in a way that was very rare especially in the world we lived in. That is what he fell in love with, but those years took such a toll on my spirit. I let my light dim so much that I didn't give myself time to discover how powerful that light could be. I never confronted the pain, and therefore never healed from it. I just kept it moving, making myself smaller, and my light not as powerful, so that I wouldn't scare the next person away. When I got to the point when I was so small that the light almost blew out, I realized I had a lot of work to do to ignite my light again.

I am grateful that now I am able to look at my father and so many others with humanity, and not through the lenses of a sad little girl. My dad died in the summer of 2016 and I wish I had more time to understand his journey from his perspective. When did his light dim? What was his story? I'll never know but I'm happy that the pain of the past is no longer determining my future. While planning his funeral, unknowingly, my stepmother revealed that she had been a part of my father's life since I was four or five years old. The realization hit me fast and hard. I was filled with anger and didn't know what to do with it. I felt so deceived because even when I thought we were a happy family, it was a lie. Then I was filled with unsurmountable guilt considering what I must have put my mother through during that time. I was captivated by my stepmother and the time she gave me, while my mother was filled with grief.

On the day of my dad's wake, I called my mother in uncontrollable tears. I apologized profusely while trying to catch my breath. She responded as she always has, with grace and comfort.

"You were a kid. A lost, sad, lonely kid trying to find your way. You have nothing to be sorry for."

Later that night at the actual wake, I got up to speak and publicly thanked my mom for being a living example of grace. I told her in front of the entire congregation that it was her grace and love throughout our journey that gave me the courage to stand up in front of everyone on that night with grace and forgiveness. It took a few months after returning home from my dad's funeral to forgive my stepmother. She was young and dumb and in love with a broken man, which caused her to make choices that did not honor her or me. I realized if I could not forgive her, I could not fully forgive myself for the choices I've made that did not honor myself or others. I chose to forgive both of us.

The level of connection I felt with my first love was very deep, and the fact that he hurt me is secondary to the fact that he helped me discover my light again. He too didn't choose me, but it wasn't because I wasn't enough. I allowed myself to believe that was the reason, but the fact is he had no idea of how to take care of the light. I had not even come fully into the light. In his own way, he recognized that, and it affected him deeply. I am grateful for this memory, and I am grateful that way back when, he saw something in me that I didn't even see in myself. Twenty plus years later he reached out to me out of the blue. His life took him on a journey as well, and he too often thought about me and the opportunity missed. He had since married three times, and this last time was with the girl that was part of our love triangle in high school. We had a wonderful conversation and I discovered he lived literally 10 minutes from my home in south Atlanta. Really? This type of thing only happens to me. We were able to discuss what happened between us, acknowledge both of our roles in why it never came to be, and get closure. I was able to ask him why he never chose me, and his answer had nothing to do with me. That was so powerful for me to hear. I was able to validate that his choices had nothing to do with my self-value. What an unexpected gift! After that conversation, I always wondered if I would bump into him since we lived so close. One day, after being at the pool all day (and looking a hot mess), I ran into my local market to get something really quick. I was on the phone with a close friend, and while looking at spaghetti sauce, glanced to my left. There he was standing at the end of the aisle. I said to my friend, "it has happened. It's him, and I gotta go." We stood there for several seconds speechless. Then one of us broke the silence. We exchanged some small talk and then parted ways. He and his wife soon moved and disappeared.

Back when I was a lost teenager, I blamed myself for why people left me, but now that I pinpointed exactly when I parked myself on the porch and when I allowed my light to dim, I've chosen a different route. I've made a choice to change the outcome of my story. That little insecure, overcompensating, perfectionist got me pretty far in life, but it was time to let her go so that I could live my life freely and authentically. I literally had to say goodbye to her and with many, many tears did just that. Today, I choose to be enough. I no longer put inaccurate meaning to the stories of my life. It wasn't until the worst thing I could possibly imagine happened to my marriage, did I even begin to realize just how much my light had dimmed. I had been yearning and searching for love so much, that I never really learned to love myself.

CHAPTER 5
LIGHT IN THE DARKNESS

"Hope is being able to see that there is light despite all of the darkness"
-Desmond Tutu

*A*t every juncture of my life, no matter how dark or gray it might have seemed, there always seemed to be a light that guided me when I needed it most. I think it is very important to find the good in all situations. Sometimes the bad things that happen have a way of overshadowing the good things, but it is those good things that give you what you need to persevere. If you think about the darkest times of your life, you can find something good that helped you make it through—a friend, a teacher, a kind stranger or a kind word. During my darkest days as a teenager, it was a family member, my father's younger brother, that kept that light from going out. My grandfather was a rolling stone, so my uncle was only nine years older than me. He has been more like a big brother than an uncle, so I will refer to him as my big brother. It is important to note the connection to my father. Perhaps, my big brother instinctively knew that he could be to me what my father was unable to be. And even deeper, it was my dad's younger brother that held his hand in his last days of life. He was the one that comforted my dad through his immense regret. It was he who assured my dad that he left an amazing legacy and that all four of his kids forgave him and loved him.

Since I could remember, I had a special connection with my big brother. In my family, we affectionately call him "Clean." As a little girl, I lit up whenever I saw him. From an early age, he referred to me as "His Angel." His presence always put a smile on my face. In our family, Clean was someone that protected us all. If someone was bothering any of the girls in our family, Clean took care of it. We all put him on a pedestal, and to be honest, we still do.

When I was around eleven years old, Clean moved away for an extended period of time, and I thought my heart would break. He was in his late teens to early twenties, and I didn't see him very often, but when I did see him, my heart melted. The thought of not seeing him, even rarely, filled me with great sadness. At that time, I didn't have much to hold on to, and my relationship with him is really the only thing that made me feel special in my crazy world. I still remember the day I had to say goodbye after my mom made him a going away dinner. I really didn't appreciate that he brought his girlfriend to the dinner, as I didn't feel as though I should have to share him when I wasn't going to see him for a long time. Needless to say, I pretended to like her and enjoyed our last evening together. And poof! He was gone.

While he was away, I was approaching my teen years, which were very challenging for me. I was experiencing the normal growing pains of that period, which were compounded with a completely dysfunctional family dynamic. I was sad, lonely, and lost. One day, feeling overwhelmingly troubled, about a week after my uncle departed, I received a letter. It started with "How is the most Beautiful Angel in the world..." Beautiful was the farthest from what I felt at that time. I was very skinny, started to experience acne, underdeveloped, and had no idea how to do my hair; but when I got that letter, I felt beautiful. I couldn't wait to write him back, and I couldn't wait to receive another letter from him. Again, it always started with "My Beautiful Angel," and I would melt each time. This was the light that kept me going when my life was very dark. It was the anticipation of these letters that brought sunshine into my days. It was like I held a special secret in my heart as I went through my daily activities. One day, instead of a letter, there was a package waiting for me. In the package was a handmade framed mirror with a picture of Clean imbedded inside that said, "Alicia you are my Ultimate Love." Needless to say, I walked around hugging that mirror day and night. Now, I was not the only person enthralled with my Uncle Brother. We all were. But you can best believe I made sure everyone knew that I was the only one that he made a mirror for. My sister and aunts quickly got tired of me and that mirror. Anyway, time passed and these letters brought me so much joy. One day I received a letter that said I am going to be coming home sooner than expected, and the first person I am going to see is my angel.

I remember it like it was yesterday. I couldn't wait for school to end, and I waited anxiously for the doorbell to ring. Sadly, the day came quickly to an end. Heartbroken that he had not come, I started to get ready for another day. I was in the shower with a shower cap on my head when the door rang. I remember my mother and sister being very excited as they opened the door, and they called me downstairs. Right away I completely panicked, because his "Beautiful Angel" looked a hot mess. I got myself together the best I could and came downstairs. I hugged him and was completely star struck. I was unable to say much at all, but I felt like the luckiest girl in the world. Clean was home and all in the world was good. Regular visits resumed. He was very handsome, so he had many girlfriends, which I wasn't thrilled about. I was just happy to hold such a special place in his heart. Sometimes this was problematic because some of the girls he dated didn't like how he put me, my sister and his sisters on a pedestal. He always made it clear from the start that if his family needed him, he was there in a heartbeat.

I was just about to turn thirteen, and he began a yearly ritual of taking me to a Broadway play and dinner for my birthday. It was something special that he only did for me and again, I took great pride in that. I would get dressed up, and it was the only time I felt beautiful from the inside out. One year he asked me what play I wanted to see. I told him, "*Dream Girls*, but it's been sold out for months." He asked my second choice and told me to be ready on our special day. I still don't know how he pulled it off at the age of twenty-something, but he not only got tickets to *Dream Girls*, we were in the first row. My entire family is tired of this story, because I still tell it like it was yesterday. Afterwards, we went to a fancy restaurant, and he taught me how to eat like a lady and taught me how a lady should be treated. He was the first male in my life to truly make me feel worthy.

As we both became adults, our relationship grew into a less fairytale connection. We became friends and began to share our real ups and downs of life. He is not perfect, and like all of us, made many mistakes as he navigated through his own life. No matter how many mistakes he made, or how hard he was on himself because of those mistakes, one thing that will never change is the impact he had on my life, and for that I will be forever grateful to him. At a very difficult time in my life, God sent me a guardian angel to give me hope in times of great pain and insecurity. Clean helped to build my self-esteem when it was at an all-time low and at such a pivotal point in my development. My dad couldn't do these things, but I now recognize that his little brother was my guardian angel and helped where my dad was unable to. As tough a period of time that was for me, it was his letters that gave me hope that everything would eventually be okay. What might have been deemed as a small gesture to others, has had an astonishing effect on me. Guess what? I still have that mirror!

Though the effect of my dad not showing up put me on the porch, those letters from Clean buried within my spirit were one of the key reasons I got the strength to figure out what was missing in my life. I had begun to feel small and almost invisible, and I knew that wasn't right. Perhaps if I didn't have this relationship and other pivotal relationships, I wouldn't have known better.

CHAPTER 6
THE UNIVERSE

"Friendship is born at that moment when one person says to another: 'What! You too? I thought I was the only one."
-C.S. Lewis

I made it through the ups and downs of high school and began college. I worked hard to get over my first love and put my dad in a separate compartment that I just didn't deal with during that time. I met one of my best friends during my sophomore year. It was her friendship that helped me uncover layers of insecurity. During this time, I was really searching for "my place," and I was at an all-time low in the confidence area. I met this totally wild, carefree, confident, smart girl that lived down the hall from me. Our first encounter was her asking me if she could put her rum punch in my fridge (the first day we moved in to the dorms). I said yes, but was thinking, "Oh Lord, what are we in for this semester?"

During this time, I felt like such an outcast. I am racially mixed (my mom is a European Jew, from Holland, and my dad is African American), and I just never felt like I fit anywhere. One evening, I was sitting outside of my dorm, and she was on her way in. She sat down and we began to talk. Instantly we had so much in common. We talked about so much that night. Similarly, she was racially mixed with Jamaican (Black) and English (White) and she talked about how she wanted to go back to Jamaica and make a difference in the government. She was very racially aware, progressive, and militant. I liked that. At this point in my life, I had not met anyone else that was of mixed heritage (and proud and okay with it), so that in itself was amazing to me. We talked for hours outside that dorm, and a friendship was made. Now, we were some match. As I stated, she was quite the free spirit, and I was not. My nickname in high school was "Laura Ingles" (from *Little House on the Prairie*), so you can imagine that many people were like, "How did these two become friends." We had become more than friends. Our souls had connected. She was the most confident and smart person I had ever met. I literally had to make mental notes of words she used, so I could look them up later. She could care less what anyone thought of her, and I cared about what everyone thought of me. I was very skinny at that time; I wore bangs to hide my forehead, and about four pairs of socks to make my legs look fatter. I was not very confident about my studies or my intelligence, but our friendship made me begin to test my own boundaries in many ways. Of course, my wild friend got me to start going to parties and pushing my hair back out of my face. This was huge for me.

She helped me to see my beauty and embrace my big forehead as part of my beauty. I stopped wearing baggy clothes and began to embrace the body that God gave me. We were both English majors, so we had some classes together, and she always sat in the front and always had something to say. As my confidence grew, I began sitting in the front, and at times I had more to say than she did, which looking back now makes me smile. She had such an impact on me and my remaining years of college. I believe she too was an angel sent to plant seeds I would later need and rely on as I got more and more courage to get off the porch. She was the first and only relationship in my life at that time where I felt I could be completely transparent and authentic. She was a non-judgment zone and continues to be to this day. She knows all my secrets! When I think about what I contributed to her, I gave her unconditional friendship. I didn't care about what she had done or what she was doing; I cared about her. As confident as she was in some areas, there were other areas that were broken and in much need of repair; it just so happened that in her weaker areas, I was strong and was able to build her up. We continue to be each other's sounding board and we still, after so many years, understand each other: the good, the bad, the ugly, and everything in between. Again, the universe sends you what you need when you need it. Her friendship made the college years amazing.

I even started dating during my senior year. He was tall, dark, and handsome, and I was tiny, skinny, and a little awkward. He saw my heart, and the beauty I still had not quite embraced. He would tell me how sexy and beautiful I was, but I was like yeah okay...but I kind of started believing him. He would encourage me to ditch the conservative clothing, and pushed me out of my fashion comfort zone. This same semester, I decided to participate in a fashion show. After I signed up, I learned that there would be a swimsuit scene and I was petrified that the world would see my underdeveloped body, which at this time had developed, but my thinking had not caught up to it yet. I did the show and the scene, and well I realized that night that my body was no longer something to be ashamed of. It was such a great show, and I loved busting through that shell. I loved the courage it took to get on that stage and overcome some of my biggest insecurities. That time of my life was filled with adventure and zest, but somewhere along the way I lost that fire. My BFF from college recently reminded me of that girl and said, "I am glad to see her emerging again."

The journey off the porch has been the scariest of my life, but it is my village that helped me through the toughest times. My sister, aunts, and best friends loved and nurtured me through it all. Once I realized how to accept help, that help was a force that continued to cheer me on as I discovered my authentic self. Some of those same relationships were challenged at the core during this time, but they all survived, and they are stronger and more real than I ever imagined possible. Getting off the porch was the best decision I've ever made!

CHAPTER 7
OUR LOVE STORY

"A real love story is sometimes exhausting. A romance is deliberately constructed to yield a certain result; the ambiguities are trimmed out, so it's neater and more pleasing to our hearts. But you don't live a love story, you live a life."
-Melissa Pritchard

After college, I dated, but it wasn't until I met my husband that my life would make a huge shift. In my early 20's, I met a young man at a cookout. The cookout was about five miles from where I'd grown up. We actually met for the first time in Atlanta a few years prior at an infamous event of the 90's called, *Freaknik*. I was underwhelmed when we first met, but he was quite persistent. After our first conversation, I sensed something different about him. We talked for hours, and began to date, but there was something about him that either scared me or gave me pause. I could not pinpoint it. We were dating for about a month, and I didn't know what was missing, so I scheduled a date with my BFF from college to meet and talk things through. I had introduced him to my family and they all loved him for me. He was dependable, handsome, and caring, but I just could not pinpoint what my spirit was telling me. She listened, and as always said to follow my heart and be honest with him. I decided to be honest and speak to him, because he was moving too fast, and I needed him to slow it down.

A week went by after we talked about slowing down, and though he still called every day, he would wait until 11pm and say I just wanted to say good night. I thought that was cute. Before we decided to slow down, I had agreed to attend a wedding with him. He asked if I was still willing to go and I said yes. We made plans to meet in Atlantic City, NJ because the bachelor party was going to be the day before. He advised that I take a bus and meet him there, so we wouldn't have two cars. We were going to stay with his brother for the weekend, so it made sense to just leave my car home. I told him, "You better be there, because I don't like depending on people and I won't have my car." He said, "Don't worry, I'll be there."

I was nervous during the whole bus ride. I didn't have my car. I wasn't familiar with Atlantic City. I was meeting someone that I just told I wanted to slow down and be friends. I expressed all of this with my BFF, and she said, "Go, it will be fine." I got to the agreed meeting spot and he was not there. I waited fifteen minutes, which quickly turned into an hour. Now panicked, I called my answering machine, but there were no messages. I called my BFF and told her what happened. All kinds of things went through my head. Maybe this was a terrible joke and that he was mad that I wanted to slow things down. I really didn't think that was true but it did run through my mind. I hung up with my BFF and went to inquire on when the bus would be heading back. They said 10 PM and it was only 4 PM at the time. I couldn't believe I was stranded in Atlantic City with my bags, and no way to get home until six hours later. After hours of waiting, I checked my answering machine once more, and there was a message from my Aunt Bonnie that said, "Call me right away, your friend has been shot." My aunt received the message because I used to hang out at her house a lot, so he had her number in his wallet. My heart sank as I dialed the number. Once I heard her voice, she calmly informed me he was okay, but that he was shot in the leg. The bachelor party had turned into a brawl and shooting. He was shot in the ankle and his tibia and fibula were shattered. My aunt gave me a number of one of the guys who was with him (the one that had called her), and they told her they would pick me up. I called him to let him know where I was, and I waited. I had not met any of his friends at this point. I was alone in a strange city waiting for a group of guys I'd never met to pick me up. My mind was spinning. I had to trust that he was the guy he presented and that his friends would be able to help me. They were very nice and upon getting in the car with them, they advised that he was okay, but that they could not take me to the hospital because they all had to go be fitted for their tuxedos as the wedding was still on. Completely discombobulated at the tuxedo store, I asked the guys for the name of the hospital. I left the fitting, and found a pay phone, and called the hospital. As soon as he heard my voice he said, "I was so worried about you." Little did he know he had me at that point, but I didn't tell him that because I still felt he had to work a little harder to earn my heart. At this point in my life, I had never experienced someone, especially a man, put me before him. The fact that the first words out of his mouth were, "I was worried about you" made me feel a sense of security I don't think I had ever felt before. He was shot and in a hospital room in overwhelming pain not knowing if he would walk again, but he was worried about me. He often jokes and says he had to get shot to earn my love. That is so not true, but it is after this shooting that our relationship grew to new levels. He took care of me from the hospital bed and made sure that I had a place to stay at his brother's house. That sense of security was like a lifeline for me. It was something I never experienced with a man. Before being taken to his brother's house by the bride and groom, I had to go to the rehearsal because there just was no time to take me before. As I sat in the church surrounded by many of his best friends, I began to sense the type of person he was. They all embraced me, and told me what a great person he was. They were all still in shock that this had happened to him. That also had a big impact on me believing in his character and that he was who he was portraying to be. Once I arrived at his brother's home, I was greeted by three beautiful kids who wanted to know who I was and everything about me. His parents, his brother, and sister-in-law also greeted me with love. I immediately felt at home and was embraced in this amazing family dynamic. My life was never the same. I drove two hours every Friday after work to see him at his brother's house. It was a magical time. He and his brother were over ten years apart and really never had the time to develop their relationship, but grew very close during his recovery. His brother's three kids adored him and they were able to develop a special connection during his recovery. We spent the first six months of our relationship in a 12' x 12' guest room. He endured several surgeries, several casts, and months of physical therapy, but he had me and an amazing family by his side the whole way.

It's something how one singular event can change the course of your life. At the time, our relationship was in its infancy. Little did we know that our life together would be solidified by one call. Upon going into the first of many surgeries, he overheard someone say, "He'll never walk again." With no insurance and several surgeries, they patched him up as best they could. Learning to walk again would take at least a year. Looking from the outside in, he seemed to be in quite a hopeless situation, and at times hopeless is what he felt. However, those times were far and few between, because though tragic as it was, so many blessings were birthed during that year of recovery. During this time, we talked about his dreams and what he wanted to do with the rest of his life. Many times, when events such as this happen, people get a new lease on life, but sometimes it fades as the injuries begin to heal. Not in his case! He told me that he wanted to make a difference in young Black men's lives. He was a finance/real estate major in college, but he wanted something different for himself and his community. The young man who shot him was seventeen or eighteen years old, and he received eighteen months. Because it was a Black-on-Black crime, the shooter was able to plea bargain. The court decided that the cost of bringing out of state witnesses back for trial was not an expense they wanted to incur. His life was forever changed, and this man would only serve 18 months. He was angry and frustrated, but once we were past the trial, he decided that he needed to forgive the man that shot him and that he needed to make a difference. Somehow, he had to be an agent of change in young lives. This was awesome to me, and I wanted to be right by his side as we changed the world. During this time, our relationship began to blossom. He had so much time on is hands. During the week, he would get down and in the dumps but by Thursday night, would start hopping around and preparing for my visit on Friday. This period of time was truly special. Not only for us but for his entire family. They were just as excited to see me when I visited, and I could not wait to get there and receive all the love that was given to me. I felt like a rock star every Friday night. It was just us and his family. He even wrote a book for me expressing how he felt about me. I recently found a journal that he kept as well, and thought wow, so much has changed.

During this time, I started to save for my own apartment and soon moved in. After about six months of recovery, his doctor appointments were farther apart, and he could return home. He did not want to return to his parent's home, so he stayed between my apartment and his brother's home for the remainder of that first year. Again, it was wonderful, but it was also just us in our own little cocoon. I realized he made me feel worthy and needed, but I don't think I felt worthy without him. Again, a theme that continued throughout my life.

Once he could walk again, he got a job as a substitute teacher. Simultaneously, he began studying for the teacher's exam and enrolled in graduate school. Upon passing his exam, he was hired as a permanent substitute teacher, and then gained employment as a fifth-grade social studies teacher. Everything he attempted, he achieved; and put 100 percent effort in. He never worked normal hours even as a substitute teacher. In that little room during his initial recovery, he also spoke about starting a basketball team at his church. He figured the team would have about ten players and they would play other community teams. He got clearance from the pastor and held tryouts one Saturday morning. Over 90 kids showed up for the tryouts, and he looked at me and told me he could not turn any of them away. This is when I believe my love for him and my belief in what he could do was solidified. Some kids came with their mothers and grandmothers who looked to him with hope in their eyes. Needless to say, instead of a team, he now had a league. Instead of just him, he had his friends and family from the same community help out as coaches, score keepers, and referees. It was an amazing and life changing opportunity for all of us. It was something bigger than us and it impacted all that were involved in this project. There were times when I looked to him frustrated and flabbergasted at how we were to pull it all off, but he never wavered and always came through. I began to believe there really was nothing he could not do, and I was honored to be his biggest supporter and cheerleader. We were a team and I believed together we could do anything. I'm not sure when he changed his mind and left me on the team alone.

Now that his career was moving in the right direction, and he was accomplishing all of the dreams we spoke about, he was ready for the next step. We got engaged on my 26th birthday. During that year, I finished my graduate degree and planned our wedding, and really believed that my life couldn't be better. We got married a year later, bought our first home, had our first baby, and his career was accelerating faster than either of us could have imagined. Upon graduating with his Master Degree in Administration, he was soon hired as an Assistant Principal, and then the youngest principal in the history of the school district that he worked. All of the dreams and aspirations that we discussed in that little room were all coming to be, and he was truly making a difference. I loved being the wind beneath his wings, and I was proud to be his wife. After our second child, I contemplated for hours upon hours on whether or not to return to work. It would be a sacrifice, but we could maintain our household with one salary. I was terrified of this choice. I knew the benefits for our kids would be tremendous but I feared losing myself in the process. In the end, I decided to be a stay-at-home mom and I don't regret one minute of that decision. However, I did, in fact, lose myself in making my husband and kids my first and only priority. I began to question who I was other than his wife and their mom, and that terrified me. But until those text messages, I may never have faced the fact that I was lost and missing from my life.

CHAPTER 8
LIFE HAPPENS

*"We must let go of the life we have planned, so as
to accept the one that is waiting for us."*
-Joseph Campbell

*A*t the height of his career, tragedy struck again, and my husband's mother, his biggest fan (besides me of course), was taken from us unexpectedly. Again, one tragic event would change the course of our life. We didn't realize how much our life changed at the absence of our matriarch. All the accolades and accomplishments just weren't the same without her here to share them. The stress and bureaucracy of being an administrator in an urban setting was beginning to take its toll. Each day was becoming harder than the last, and I could feel things changing, but I really did not know how to help him or us. By now, we had our third child, and we decided that a fresh start would be best especially since the real estate market was at its height. He always planned to go back to Atlanta, and now seemed like the right time to do it. He got a job as a principal in another urban setting so we bought a house and moved south. I was excited about the move because at this point, my older sister and mother had moved to Florida, and my husband's mother passing away left us less attached to New Jersey. The only apprehension I had was that Atlanta was a familiar place for him and the behaviors (drinking and hanging out) that terrified me. I somehow feared that he would succumb to old pressures and old behaviors simply by being there. Perhaps I pushed him to those behaviors because I was relentless in trying to keep my family from those dangers. I held on tight and the tighter I held, the more I came to realize there was nothing I could do to stop what was destined to happen. I thought that I could keep all negative influences out and protect our cocoon, but that really was unrealistic and put all of us in a constant space of rigidity.

Everything appeared fine on the outside, but on the inside, neither of us was okay. We didn't understand it and therefore, had no idea of what to do about it. So, we existed in the realm of perfection, but the cracks in the foundation were growing. For my husband, the joy that once came from being an administrator was replaced with an overwhelming gloom. I watched as the internal struggle and pain overtook him both physically and mentally as he began to realize he wasn't happy in his role. In fact, he was miserable. I was still a stay-at-home mom and he felt that he had no other choice but to do what he had to do to support his family. Again, God had a different plan and another tragedy would soon hit hard. He was let go without warning from being a principal, and he had to tell me this news.

He called me while I had five kids in my car (mine and my nieces). I hear the words, "I was let go," and my head started spinning. I knew I had to jump into supportive wife mode, so I told him we will be okay and we could talk more when he got home. I got off the phone so I could breathe and think. I called my aunt, then fell apart. She listened, validated my fears, and told me to get it together and that he needed me now more than ever. I was so scared. How would we make it? We were already sacrificing financially, and now we would have no income. I couldn't show him these fears, because he needed me more than ever to help rebuild his spirit. His spirit was broken before the termination, but now he was filled with self-doubt and failure. I cried, then got myself together and went into "save my family" mode. I found different scriptures and posted them around the house. I listened to all of his ideas of alternative careers. We worked together to update his resume, and I supported any and everything he wanted to do, but his spirit was broken and that I did not know how to fix. I would go walking, and cry hysterically, because I was terrified but I never revealed that to him. I just kept being his rock and encourager.

One night, I could not sleep so I got on the computer and started looking for jobs at colleges that might be of interest to him. He was resistant to these positions because the pay was substantially lower, but his passion was for students, and I knew that. This particular night there was a posting for a position at the college he attended for undergrad. I read the job description and immediately recognized that this was the perfect position for him. I updated his resume and cover letter. I printed out the job and gave it to him to review the next day. I could see that his interest was piqued, but he was still resistant because of the pay. I told him to forget about the pay and just go for it. That's what he did and together we put everything we had into him getting the interview for this job. I knew if he got the interview, he would get the job. I believed in him that much! He did get the interview and he did get the job. On his way to the final interview he called and said he knew he was going to get the job. He said, God spoke to him in the car and he knows this is where he is supposed to be. I felt the weight of the world lift from my shoulders. I felt like I got my husband back, and my life was perfect again. During this same period of time, I was offered a position and was back in the workforce. It was great timing, because it was time for me to get back out there, but I had been a stay-at-home mom for so long that it was a scary step. Now that I was back to work, my kids were good, we survived financial ruin with the help of my family, we were back on track! Or were we?

Like with his previous career, he became consumed again with this new challenge. Though he was happier in this new position, and I wanted to believe in that perfect picture again, it wasn't the same. We weren't the same and I was terrified of what was missing; but we pretended that all was okay for years. The picture of our family that we built appeared perfect, but the cracks were beginning to spread and because we both desperately loved the picture, we ignored the cracks until we couldn't any longer.

CHAPTER 9

WHEN THE DRESS GETS TOO TIGHT

*"Sometimes you find yourself in the middle of
nowhere, and sometimes in the middle of nowhere,
you find yourself."*

-Anonymous

One day while out walking with my workout partner and friend, she shared a story with me about a couple that was very close to her. The couple split and the wife left her kids with their father without warning. My friend was extremely upset because this was a couple with which she was very close. It was surprising. Later, after she understood more of the story, she discovered that the wife had been struggling for some time. The wife described her pain and said her life had become like wearing a dress that no longer fit. She began to feel so uncomfortable that the dress was beginning to squeeze the life out of her. As my friend was talking, I could not help but to empathize with this poor woman. I was beginning to feel so uncomfortable in my life and had no idea what to do about it. While I could not imagine leaving my kids, I could not judge her because I realized the amount of pain she must have been in to make the decision to not only leave, but leave her kids behind. It had to be deeply tormenting. I felt her pain.

Remember my deal breaker during pre-marital counseling was alcohol abuse? My husband was a heavy drinker in college and in his early 20's, and I had heard many stories about how he behaved when he drank alcohol. When we got married, he had given up drinking because somehow he linked the tragedy of his shooting with the fact that they were all drinking. So, the foundation of our relationship was built during a time when he didn't drink at all. During counseling, the pastor approached this topic as much as possible, but you don't know what you don't know. About three years after we were married, he went out with friends and didn't return home until the early morning. This was not something I was accustomed to and not what we agreed to. He had gone out and got so drunk that he couldn't find his way home before morning. This started to happen once or twice a year, and I blamed his friends for being a bad influence. I got upset, but I got over it. What choice did I have? Each time it happened, he promised me it would never happen again. But it was just a matter of time before it happened again, and again. I wrote him letters. I warned him that each time he did this it was chipping away from the trust I had in him and the love I had for him. I warned him that one day the chipping away would destroy us. I don't really think he believed it would. Why would he?

I only talked and never took action or required more. Not his fault, but he believed I would always be there. I would always get over it. That was our pattern year after year. He was great in many other ways, so the binge drinking, occasional lies, not coming home until the morning leaving me to wonder if he is alive or dead on the road somewhere shouldn't matter so much. I convinced myself that this was okay, but each one of those times left me with a deep feeling of fear and emptiness.

Since moving to Atlanta, I always felt like the rug would be pulled from underneath my feet, and I would fall so hard that I would not recover. My family was everything to me, so my response to that fear was to hold on tight to my life as I knew it. I tried to control everything: him, my kids, and our entire environment. I held on so tightly to a world I could not imagine losing. I did everything in my power to keep everything and everyone I perceived as harmful to our family out, and in doing so I made huge mistakes. I missed things with my kids, I missed things in my marriage, and I lost myself completely. After the blow of the text messages, I realized that as much as I tried to control and protect, it didn't work. In fact, now that I was in the phase of understanding where I was, I found an old email that I sent my husband after one of his binge drinking episodes from at least four years earlier. I sat and read the email, and I literally could have sent the same email, at that very moment, because nothing had changed. I was stunned that I was in the same space year after year, accepting the same behavior, and allowing myself to fade into the background. I vowed after reading that email that I would not be in the same place anymore. I was ready to be different and live differently, and that would require him to do the same, or not, but I knew I could not wear a dress that did not fit any longer. The discomfort was becoming unbearable.

CHAPTER 10

WHEN THE BUBBLE POPS

"Look within. Within is the fountain of good, and
it will ever bubble up, if thou wilt ever dig."
-Marcus Aurelius

emember the text messages, and my resolve that I would no longer give one hundred percent to the relationship. I really had no idea what that would mean for me or how it would change my life, but I would find out over the next several months and even years. At the time, all I knew for certain was that something drastically changed inside me. I had been with my husband for 18 years at that point (15 years married, and 3 years prior to marriage). For those entire 18 years, I was completely devoted and dedicated to him, his dreams, and my children. I was closed to anything or anyone that could interfere with this magical "world" we created. There were many signs along the way that we had some serious underlying issues, but I was way too scared and stubborn to face that reality, so I didn't. But now, I decided to allow myself to live outside of that commitment. I had no other choice but to navigate outside of the safe little bubble that I created. It was scary, yet quite exciting at the same time. I was learning who I was again, and sometimes didn't recognize the person staring back at me in the mirror.

What I began to realize was that the bubble transcended far beyond just my marriage. For a good portion of my life, my main focus was being the best for everyone in my life. If there was a role I was given, I wanted to be the best at it. When your focus is on being the best for everyone else, learning to be the best for you is not only foreign but almost unfathomable. I was the ultimate rule follower and people pleaser, and the rules were clear to me: be good, don't disappoint, and be the best. There was little room for error or balance. Be perfect to and for everyone at any cost. Don't get me wrong, I loved being the best wife, mother, daughter, sister, niece, best friend, but somewhere along the way I lost myself. I never learned or desired how to be the best me for me. Somehow I perceived that as selfish. Given that, I put my all into everyone else. When some of those relationships began to fail, I had to take a close look at myself. Sure, I could blame them, but what was really going on was that I didn't believe I was enough or worthy of real authentic relationships. I didn't believe that I deserved what I gave to others, so I never gave to myself what I gave to others. I placed very high expectations on myself and in turn expected more from others than they were able to give. That was okay though because I would make up for anything they weren't able to give, after all, that was my job, right? I created a world in which I lived my safe, pretty life. If I didn't give people a chance to disappoint me, maybe I wouldn't get disappointed. WRONG. And boy did I realize how human I was when I continued to fall short or disappoint some of my closest friends. When you seek perfection, imperfection hits you like a ton of bricks. It took me years, decades, to realize the bubble I created was far from safe. It was so fragile and it could pop at any moment, so that meant I lived in fear for most of my adult life. Fear that I would do or say something that wasn't perfect, and it would all just fade away; fear that someone else would do or say something that would ruin what I deemed as perfect. I became the fixer. I couldn't shake the feeling that one day the rug would be pulled from under me, and I would fall so hard that I wouldn't be able to get up, so I fought like hell to stay on solid, safe ground.

On that October 6th evening, the thing I feared most happened, and in the thirty seconds it took for me to read that text message, the bubble popped, the rug was pulled, and I fell hard! In that moment, I thought it was the worst thing that could ever happen to me. How would I ever recover? My disappointment was so deep. My fear that I would not recover was even deeper. When did I become this weak little girl? At this point of deep despair, I began to slowly look inside of myself (which my husband had suggested) and I realized I had unrealistic standards for most of the people in my life, but more importantly, unrealistic standards for ME. I found myself feeling let down and empty every time someone didn't live up to my expectations. In turn, I felt inadequate and like a failure, because it must have been something I did that hindered them from living up to their promises. I didn't love them enough, or talk to them enough, or I must have let them down in some way, I must have said the wrong thing, or I must have done something to make them not love me enough, because I sincerely believed, I alone wasn't enough for the love I desired. It had to be my fault.

My light bulb moment that year happened when I realized that the bubble I created, though real on so many levels, was an image that I created so that I would not have to deal with the dangers that might be lurking outside of the bubble. I created a safe place where I could not be hurt anymore. But was it really safe? Was it really okay to live in fear? Again, my husband's advice to look within was never far from my mind. I asked myself if I was as happy as I thought? Was I fulfilled? Or was I just safe, until I wasn't safe anymore? As I began to navigate life with this new perspective in my marriage, I began to slowly answer those questions. This was mind-blowing, because in my bubble, I didn't allow myself to even consider these types of questions. Of course I was happy and fulfilled! Wasn't I supposed to be? Look at my Christmas picture and letter, we look and sound perfect. When I got the courage to honestly ask and answer the questions, what I found out was that I lived in fear and played it safe for most of my life. I took the safe career route. I married a man that offered a safe, secure life. I maintained safe friendships trying desperately not to disappoint. I started to question whether or not any of the things I worked so hard to maintain were real. As scary as it was to face this question, I had to find out. I wanted real. I wanted raw. I wanted honesty. I was terrified, but I yearned for it. So, I dug deep and found the courage to step back. I stepped back to see if I didn't do everything to make all okay for everyone, what would happen? This was so frightening! What if they don't step up? Who is going to fill in the gaps? What if the relationship isn't what I thought it was? What if my heart gets broken? What if I can't make it all better again? These were real questions, and I didn't know how I would survive if these relationships weren't what I thought or hoped they were. How could I possibly survive the disappointment? More importantly, why did I allow myself to get here in the first place? That was the scariest of all the questions, and I knew at some point I would have to answer it.

As I began to slowly step back and let go of being in control of these relationships, I began to realize that not only was I overcompensating in my marriage, but in most of the relationships I held near and dear to my heart. I lived in constant fear of disappointing others and didn't know how being true to my own desires or thoughts felt. I let the bubble pop and this is where the journey of discovering the authentic Alicia began...

CHAPTER 11

RUNNING SAVED MY SOUL

*"Running teaches us to keep moving forward, one
step at a time, especially in the most painful
moments."*
                                            -runwicki.org

*D*uring the first year after the text messages, though I
was discovering new parts of me, I fell into a
slump. I felt paralyzed and a real depression began to
surface. I had read somewhere that walking could help, so I
decided to try it. One day, I read that if you just put your
sneakers on and take the first step, you will keep on going. I
decided I needed to take the first step. I put my sneakers on,
listened to some inspirational music, and began walking.
The first day was somewhat of a chore. Then, as I went more
and more, it became therapeutic, almost like a drug. I began
to need it and then one day I felt like running. There is a
huge, steep hill in front of my home, and when we moved to
this community, I wasn't even able to walk half way up that
hill. On this particular day when I set out to do my walk, I
decided to see how far I could run up the hill. I made it
about half way. The next time I went out, I decided to go
just a little bit further. Each time I went out, I kept adding a

little more distance to the run, and before I knew it I was running up and down the entire hill. This is where my love of running set in. This is where I discovered my strength, my tenacity, and my toughness. This is where I discovered that running would become a metaphor for my life. It was during my runs that I found clarity. It was where I saw myself as strong and not that weak little girl looking for approval. It was where, even when I felt like I could go no farther, that I dug deep and took a few more steps. It is where I challenged myself to do more and be more. Now that I could run the hill, I asked my dear friend and workout partner to join me in another challenge. I wanted to run my first 5k, but I knew I needed her support and commitment as well. We had become that source of encouragement for each other in fitness and in life, and I wanted to take this journey with her (another angel strategically placed in my life). She agreed and we trained for our first 5K. Ironically, I completed the race in a great time for a first timer, and the race was one year after that infamous night in October when I came across those text messages.

The strength and confidence that I gained through running began to transfer into every aspect of my life. I allowed myself to feel that strength and confidence and started caring more about my appearance. I allowed myself to feel pretty, sexier, and started to push myself to do more things out of my comfort zone. People started to take notice, and I was offered a promotion at work. I had always been on the backend/operations of the company but was given the opportunity to be in front of clients. This excited and terrified me at the same time. It would require travel, and lots of public speaking and training of large groups of people. My absolute BIGGEST fear was PUBLIC SPEAKING, but like that hill in front of my house, I knew I had to conquer it. I needed this. I needed to grow more and more. Growing had become infectious for me and I didn't want to stop.

Also during that year of exploration, I met a new friend that became very dear to me. He too was married and felt a huge disconnect with his wife and began to pursue a friendship with me. This was new to me, because I would not have even noticed his advances had I still been in my bubble, but now I was flattered that he was showing me attention. It felt good, even though in my heart I knew it was wrong. He too was searching for something deeper within himself. We became friends, and that friendship grew into much more than friends. We were both emotionally desperate for more. Initially, we developed an emotional dependency for each other. He offered me a lifeline. I see now it followed my pattern. When my dad rejected me as a teen, Clean was my lifeline. When my husband betrayed me, I found a lifeline in the form of connection with another man. I continued to put Band-Aids® on the pain, instead of dealing with it head on. I never healed from any of the heartache that dwelled in my heart. I didn't plan for our friendship to evolve so deeply, but if I didn't have it, I'm not sure if I could have survived the level of emotional rejection I was receiving from my husband. My heart was broken, and being seen and heard took over my desire to do the right thing.

Needless to say, the dichotomy between my husband ignoring my heart and my friend engaging me fully caused complication. The realization that my husband, who was supposed to be my best friend and soulmate, was incapable of connecting with my heart was devastating. Now that I had gotten to know myself on a whole new level, I wanted him to see me through a different lens. I wanted him to see this person that had emerged. I had finally found the courage to explore the response my husband gave over a year ago after finding the text messages. He'd suggested I look within myself to see what might be missing or what I could do differently. I did just that and started looking within and realized I overcompensated so much in our relationship; I deprived myself of connection, engagement, and genuine friendship. I was different now, and I wanted to give him a chance to be there. I desperately wanted him to see the new me. I was less uptight. I was fun. I was less controlling and rigid, because I realized I was holding on too tight to live fully. I had to reach him! I expressed to him that I wanted to feel his heart. I wanted more for us. I still believed that I had the power to fix us. I talked to him expressing what was missing for me and asked what was missing for him. His answer was always that he wanted more sex. At the time, I anxiously wanted to fix us so I tried to meet him where he was and give him more sexually, thinking that if I gave him what he expressed he needed, he would in turn, give me what I needed. That didn't happen and each sexual encounter began to leave me feeling empty and invisible. What I needed was a connection beyond the physical. Unfortunately, this was something he either could not do or perhaps was incapable of doing. Thinking about it now, I lost him a long time ago, but I was blind to what it was or when it happened. The text messages were the blow, but he had betrayed our marriage well before I encountered those text messages, and the level of betrayal was far bigger than I could have imagined. The truth is, I could have forgiven him for everything, if he was willing to figure out where we went wrong. If he was willing to be honest and acknowledge all he had done, and sincerely wanted to seek help. We were broken, but if he was willing to dig deep I was willing to work through it. He wasn't, so I sought to fix my broken heart with someone who saw it.

My husband told me I was his best friend. He had shared more with me than anyone else in his life. Perhaps he thought that should be enough. I tried to understand what kept him stuck and unable to take any action. He continued to wait me out, and I guess he thought it would eventually disappear, because in the past, I would go back to overcompensating and fix (on the outside) what was broken. This time was different though. There was no turning back for me, and though I didn't want to lose him or all that we created together, I just couldn't pop back into the bubble. I tried for years but that dress I was wearing was getting smaller and smaller. Wearing it had gotten so painful at this point. I had grown at least two sizes and it was much too small for me now. I tried talking to him, writing to him, crying to him, praying for him. I even tried texting him. I still wanted him to see this new me that was emerging. I wrote blog posts about my journey, hoping he would read them and gain access to my heart and want to at least discuss what I had written, but each month I waited and got little to no feedback. Each time I dug for more and searched for what he needed, the response I always got was, "we are good" or "stop worrying so much." He wanted more sex, and if he got that, he was good. What he never noticed was I was far from good with us and becoming increasingly good with *me*. I was not worrying so much as I was moving forward without him each day that he ignored me and our disconnect. I was drifting farther and farther away from him, but he refused to acknowledge or face that reality. I believe he was emotionally paralyzed and stuck in what was, refusing to see that I was no longer to put up with the deception or disconnection. It seemed like he wanted that perfect girl who would do whatever it took to make that picture work. It felt like he wanted me to suck it up and be smaller so the little dress could fit again. The cost on my heart—my soul, really didn't matter. The picture, it seemed in his eyes, was worth saving at any cost. What he did not recognize was that I discovered a new energy toward life. My vision for myself was far too expansive to fit back into a perfect little picture, no matter how pretty the picture appeared. The fear of losing myself again, became more important to me than preserving the picture. This was the beginning of such a tough journey. I didn't want to lose him or my family, so I continued to wait and pray that things would change. However, the conflict within my spirit was so strong. The need for growth, change, and expansion was stirring inside of me. It became so uncomfortable in our space. We were fighting for different things: He was fighting for what was, and I was fighting for what could be. The next couple of years were so very challenging until ultimately, I chose me.

CHAPTER 12

PEACHTREE ROAD RACE

"The freedom to be yourself is a gift only you can give yourself. But once you do, no one can take it away. "

-Doe Zantamata

On July 4, 2012, I decided to run the infamous Peachtree Road Race. It was the hottest summer I had ever experienced in Atlanta. I trained for the race, hydrated with coconut water the day before, and ate pasta. As prepared as I was, I was not prepared enough. As I crossed what I thought was the finish line, I could not understand why everyone was still running. The finish line that I crossed was just the photo op line. The real finish line was about .01 miles ahead and as I began to run again, things became foggy. I started seeing people on either side of me making sure I was okay, and then I woke up in a medical tent. I was somewhat delirious. I started looking for my friends that ran the race with me, but I was all alone with a very nice red headed nurse. As I lay there, my life as it was started to flash before my eyes. I felt this overwhelming need to tell the nice nurse everything. I'm not catholic, but I felt the need to confess. I stared at her and felt a sense of freedom I hadn't experienced before. I put my hands on her cheeks, and brought her head closer to mine. I bravely stated, "I need to tell you something," and I confessed everything. I told her about my affair. I told her that my marriage was over and my husband had no idea. I told her that my heart was lonely. I told her everything! Poor thing! By the end of my confession, she was as white as a ghost. Then I asked her if I had finished the race. She didn't know, so I assumed I hadn't and started crying. How could I not have finished when I was so close! I was devastated. After a while, my husband, girlfriend, and kids found me, but I was angry and sad, and still quite despondent. My husband yelled at me to drink water and his voice annoyed me. I was still quite out of it and very irritable. His voice and presence there stole my freedom and I felt so deflated. My girlfriend knows me well and though she did not quite understand where I was, she knew I needed something different in that moment. She told my husband to let her take over, and she gently held my hand, and wiped the smeared black mascara off my face. She encouraged me to drink water and I sat up and began to respond to her. I was very aggravated with my husband although he hadn't actually done anything. When I was alone with the red head, I felt freedom. When my husband came, I felt like that dress was confining me and I had to suck it in. Once I started to get myself together, the red head said to my husband and girlfriend, "She is something else. What a personality she has." My girlfriend smiled and said, "Yes she is," and my husband began to make excuses for my behavior saying, "She only acts like that if she's had a couple of drinks." This infuriated me. I was free and she thought I was "something else" dammit. Stop trying to fit me into a damn little box! I didn't say those words, but that was how I felt. The freedom I experienced with the red head was a freedom for which I yearned. I wanted to be authentic and "something else," not inhibited and boring.

Later that evening, my girlfriend called me and said very excitedly, "you finished the race." I was still in pretty bad shape but those words made everything better. It gave me hope and courage for my life. The race once again mirrored where I found myself. The next day there was video coverage of the race. I was able to watch myself in those last three minutes of the race. When my legs started to wobble, two volunteers came on both sides of me. Each held my arm in theirs and walked me across the finish line before I collapsed in one of their arms. Seeing that made me realize I would see my way off the porch and into my authentic life, even if I needed a little help making it over the finish line. That freedom I felt with that red head was not something that I could forget and that desire fueled me every day.

PART TWO

DISCLOSING ALICIA

CHAPTER 13
SEARCHING FOR ANSWERS

"A journey of a thousand miles begins with a single step."

-Lau-Tzu

After eighteen years of marriage, deciding that it is over is HUGE and devastating. I never imagined my life with anyone but my husband and our beautiful family. Things happen in a marriage. I could go down a list of offenses that my husband did to lead me to that decision, and he probably could do the same. However, the main reason my marriage ended is because I changed. I chose me. I believe my husband loved me as best as he knew how, shared more with me than anyone else in his life, and would stay with me until death did us part. That is what we promised and vowed to do. His happiness and even my happiness were secondary to the promise. That is what still causes me sadness because had I not changed the rules, I would be able to do what I vowed to do. However, he changed the rules too. And because he did, I was forced to find myself in the confines of my "beautiful life." On that beautiful wedding day, I didn't know what or who I would become, what my needs would be, how I yearned to be seen and heard, or how I would overcompensate for all that was missing as to not be left alone. After discovering the betrayal of infidelity, I let it all unravel. My heart, my soul, my needs, my wants, and I accepted everything that was revealed. Living in fear that someone wouldn't love me the way I yearned and overcompensating for those needs, led me to a very lonely existence. Feeling lonely in a life that appeared perfect was heartbreaking. After the Peachtree Road Race, I decided to change. I did everything in my power to bring my husband along on this growth journey with me, but he didn't appear to want to change. He seemed content just the way things were, and when it was clear I was no longer content, I believe he began to resent me. What he didn't realize was that I had no choice but to change. I was dying inside. I knew from the very beginning of our relationship that I was what he needed. He told me that. His friends told me that. Eventually, even his mother told me that. In my twenties, I loved being needed. I loved that being with me made him want to be better. I loved that role, and as he began to really soar in accomplishing his goals and dreams, I took great pride in being his rock and his partner. As my life took a huge turn, I wondered if he would be the same for me. The truth is not that he couldn't, but I never gave him the chance because I was afraid he would not show up, and my heart could not survive that again. Or at least, that is what I told myself. I took a big breath and stepped back. I told him what I needed, and prayed he would step up to the plate. He didn't know what to do, because I never taught him how to love me since I never fully loved myself. I wanted desperately for him to figure it out but he had no clue or desire to do this, so he did nothing.

The three years that followed that monumental night in October were filled with self-exploration. I continued to try and pull my husband along, but because I always snapped back into my familiar role, I think he felt it was safer to just wait me out. After all, he and my kids have been my everything for all of our life together. Unfortunately, he was very wrong. He would say things like, "I am working on me" and "I am trying to figure out what you want," and every time he would say these words that were not supported by action, I would drift farther and farther away from the life that he was so secure in. In the past, words worked for him. They were enough for me to give it one more try. I am a writer. I believe in words. But when there was no action to support the words, they became empty. I resented his words. I trusted the little voice inside of me that was speaking to me all along. I began to talk to God all day and every day. I would ask for direction or signs for what I should do or if he was genuine, and every time I prayed, the universe would answer.

CHAPTER 14

LIVING A DOUBLE LIFE

"One of the happiest moments ever is when you find the courage to let go of what you can't change."

-Anonymous

Although the Peachtree Road race had come and gone, the freedom I felt with the nurse was never far away. I started living two lives. There was the life I had with my husband and my kids where I pretty much did everything for everyone. If they noticed a difference, I wasn't aware. Then, there was the life I lived when I worked and traveled. In that life, I was free, adventurous, witty, sexy, fun, selfish, and alive. I gave myself permission to explore this new side of me. As liberating as it was, I knew the other relationship was inappropriate. No, I knew it was downright wrong, but at that time I didn't care. My husband's disconnection felt like rejection and the pain was deep, so this is how I justified my indiscretion. As time passed however, even that relationship wasn't enough. I spent a lot of time in turmoil because this was also not the life I wanted. I hated the level of deception. I was terrified of the exposure, but if it happened we would have no other option but to address the growing gap in our marriage, right? Eventually my extramarital affair was uncovered, and my husband had no choice but to address it.

One morning he asked me directly, "How close are you with this friend of yours? Is something going on?" I now had a choice, and it took a great deal of courage to choose to tell the truth. I admitted that he was more than just a friend. As the words came out, my head started racing and I felt overcome with shame and guilt. I went down a road I never thought possible for me. I judged women like me. I was the victim of infidelity and here I was, a participant. A part of me was also relieved that it was finally out there. I'd been checked out of my marriage and he finally noticed. So here I was in an unfamiliar, messy space and it was so unlike me, but bam! There it was. I'm sure a thousand thoughts crossed through my husband's head. My stomach was in knots as I looked at him sitting on the floor with his head in his hands.

He knew the magnitude of what it meant for me to invest myself in someone else! I believe both his heart and ego were crushed in that moment. Similarly, as I felt with the realization of his infidelity, he now was forced to acknowledge that the cracks in our marriage were deepening. My loyalty and dedication to him and my family was something he was completely secure in, and now that was gone. One would think that it was clear of just how much I had transformed from being his perfect little wife. I began to wonder if he would fight for me? If he would fight for our family? If he would fight for himself?

After my admission, we talked very little. I felt like my world was spinning out of control. I had only shared my secret with a handful of people. People I could trust not to judge me. I felt horrible that I hurt my husband so deeply. It was as though my world was falling apart and I wasn't sure I could handle it. So, I ran away. I called my sister and told her I needed to get away. I did not tell her yet what was going on, but she suspected something had happened. I spent the weekend with her, and she actually asked, "What are you running away from?" I was not ready and did not have the courage to share with her what was going on. Her respect and love was not something I was ready to risk. I spent the weekend reflecting. I did not want to lose my marriage, so I told my husband that I would limit interaction with my friend. He seemed to accept my words and never brought it up again. I was a little perplexed that he did not demand that I never see him again. I was confused that he didn't want to delve deeper into the details of what I had done or the implications for our marriage. I was fearful that our life together would be in shambles but I returned home and it appeared as though the conversation had never happened. The void and distance between us grew wider.

Another year passed and nothing came of the exposure, so my friend reemerged and pursued the relationship again. I let him in and I justified it because my husband gave me no indication that he gave a shit. The fact that it was wrong didn't matter either because it gave me a life preserver, and without it I feared I would drown. So, without even realizing it, I parked myself on another porch in another codependent relationship with a person who was incapable and unavailable to care for my heart. Now, here's a clear pattern. I was still playing it small and settling for less than I wanted and less than I deserved. I still did not believe I was worthy of more from any relationship.

By December 2013, I felt like I was coming apart at the seams. I knew I could not stay in this space much longer. I was managing two relationships and neither were filling the insurmountable void that was growing within me. Desperate for answers, I began seeing a counselor early that November. I went to the counselor about my marriage and told her I was seeking clarity. During the first session, I explained to her where I was in my marriage and I shared with her the relationship outside of my marriage. From that point on, she would not counsel me on anything except the affair. I grew quite frustrated with her. I wanted to scream and say look at me. Hear me. But she insisted that I could not get clarity as long as the relationship outside of my marriage existed on any level. After one of our scheduled sessions, I left angry. I decided I didn't like her and that she didn't know what she was talking about. By this time, I had shared my secret life with my sister and to my surprise, she didn't judge me. My sister was there for me as always, but also saw the torment that this relationship was causing me. Though she didn't agree with the counselor's style, she did agree that the relationship wasn't healthy and that it was blurring my vision on what I needed to do with my marriage. Deep down, I knew they were right but I had become so dependent on the relationship to save me from my despair. I wasn't sure that I could do this by myself. I had big decisions to make as the year was coming to an end and the realization of eminent changes sent me into an abyss of tears. My family was in another room, and had no idea of the space I was in. I cried uncontrollably through the night, anguished by my situation.

In late December, our family took a road trip to New Jersey (our home state). It was a trip we had taken many times as a family. On the outside, we looked the same to all that loved us, but on the inside, we were farther apart emotionally than we had ever been. During the trip, my husband noticed my distance, which was also turning into resentment, and said to me one morning, "You have already left me." That broke my heart, but in so many ways it was true. When we returned to Atlanta, I would have to face both relationships head on. It was time for my husband and I to go deep and answer the hard "whys" of where we were. And it was time for me to end my other relationship—for good this time.

As a Christmas gift, my niece gave us a gift certificate to a swanky restaurant in the city. My husband and I decided to use it and go on a dinner date in the first week of January 2014. Dinner started off nice, but distant. I didn't plan on the evening ensuing the way it did as the conversation that transpired was the beginning of our end. We started talking about our goals for the new year and before long I brought up our marriage. I also brought up the affair. During the discussion, I must have crossed a line when I told him, "I don't regret it." I continued to talk without realizing the effect that those words had on him. Shortly after I said them, while in mid-sentence, he got up from the table and walked away. He said he could not look at me and that he wanted to hit something. As I sat at the table, nervous, anxious, uncomfortable, I was actually also hopeful because he showed some emotion and that he was bothered. I thought, now we can really get somewhere (I was still on the porch...hoping...waiting). We left the restaurant and on the drive home, I tried to explain to him why I did not regret it, but I don't think he could get past the actual word *regret*. I have a horrible relationship with that word. I told him, "You have regretted every time you lied to me, stayed out all night drinking and cheating, but regret did absolutely nothing to prevent you from doing it again. I don't want your regret! I want your growth. I want your ability to figure out why you do or did the things you've done time after time. I want us to really work on what is broken, because clearly we both turned to others to fill the voids we were experiencing at home. I don't regret it because I've figured out why. I've grown from the experience, and I am a better person because it happened. I hate that my actions have caused you pain, embarrassment, and shame, but it was never my intent to hurt anyone. My heart was lonely and I was vulnerable." We talked for hours and at the end of the conversation, he said, "I'm glad we talked, because I have confidence and trust that you will now do the right thing."

I was flabbergasted! Did he really think one conversation would fix us?

"You shouldn't trust me."

He threw his hands in the air as if to say, what the hell do you want?

"My heart and soul are no more filled than they were before we started this conversation. I am still lonely, lost, and vulnerable, so, no, you should not trust me."

I once put so much pride into being a good girl and always doing the right thing but now it angered me that he wanted to put me back in that box. I AM HUMAN. I HAVE NEEDS. LOOK AT ME. These basic desires became so much more important to me than being anyone's good girl ever again.

The next morning, I left for a trip and it was now time to face my other relationship head on. I decided if I was going to really attempt to sort out my life, the counselor was right. I had to be brave and I had to face it alone. I allowed myself to replace the pain of one with another that was just as toxic. I had to figure out my life! I called and told him I needed to end the relationship for real this time. No contact. No talking. No nothing. The pain was enormous because I was terrified to be alone again, but the desire to fix my life was bigger than the fear. As I hung up the phone, I literally could not breathe. I began to feel like my life was spinning out of control. Alone in my hotel room, I called my sister frightened and unnerved. I could hardly get the words out, "I...can't...breathe." I'm not sure how she did it, but within a matter of minutes, room service knocked on the door and delivered hot tea. She calmly helped me catch my breath and talked me through what had just happened. It felt like I had just jumped off a cliff, and I was so afraid to face my life and all that was ahead of me.

Heading home on the plane all I felt was numb. My sister was amazing the night before as she jumped in to save me from hitting the bottom off the cliff, but it was clear that I was confused and scared. I had no idea how to navigate my life and what it had become. I felt so alone and scared of what would unfold as I faced my marriage. However, I did know that what was most important at this point of my journey was for me to start the process of loving myself. The patterns of unworthiness had to stop and finding the courage to face the fear and pain was the beginning of that process. On the flight home I was overwhelmed with sadness and wrote the following passage:

"I'm on the plane. The battery on my iPad just died so I can't read, and candy crush is not working on my phone for some reason. So, I'm left to the many thoughts that continue to swim through my mind. I would have preferred to stay lost in the story of someone else's dysfunctional life than my own. I am seriously thinking about leaving my marriage, and I find myself contemplating things at one time I thought could not be possible. I made my husband and my kids my entire life for 17+ years, and now I find that I am a stranger in my own life. At some point, I allowed myself to get a glimpse of me separate from them, and I haven't been able to fit back in the box. Nor do I want to. My husband is not the guy I thought he was. Actually, he is, which makes this so hard. He showed me the man he wanted to be all those months in that little room, and in many ways, he has lived up to a lot of it, but there is a

dark, shady side that continues to show itself, and has led me to a place of distrust.

My heart has been ignored, I've been deceived, and lied to, and that was never part of the deal...or better yet...vows. I've never wanted to give up on him, or our marriage, but I feel that God has shown me so many signs that he is who he is...and my heart has closed its door. I don't know what it would take to turn this around without me losing myself again and any chance of finding peace and joy in my life. I've surrendered it all to God, so I know that won't happen. God and I won't allow it. I want to see my kids, but I am dreading going home. I'm forced to put on a facade of normalness, when every fiber inside of me is quite uncomfortable. I'm trapped for now in a life that is not what it appears to be, and I have to make everything on the outside look okay for my sweet babies who rely so heavily on everything being "okay." I feel like I'm wearing a dress that is much too tight, and at any moment it could fall apart at the seams. I feel strong and clear one moment, and sad and lonely the next. I feel like I am in a race by myself and though I have so many cheering me along...I'm scared, lonely, tired, weary, hurting, lost, and have so far to go to the finish line.

Sometimes I feel like passing out like at the road race just to give my soul a break. It hurts too much to *continue, and the tears won't stop flowing, so I will stop now.*

CHAPTER 15
SLIDING DOOR MOMENTS

"Occasionally, weep deeply over the life you hoped would be. Grieve the losses, then wash your face. Trust God. And embrace the life you have."
-John Piper

*I*t was January 2014, and I told my husband during that long talk before I left, that we could not be in the same place a year from now. After returning home from my trip, I fell into a deep depression for about a week. I experienced an overwhelming despair. My husband noticed that I was not myself since returning and asked why. I gave a generic response. He tried to dig for more, but gave up pretty quickly. I've always been terrified to stay down too long, so I picked myself up, put my sneakers on and ran to begin to clear my mind. I began to navigate this completely uncomfortable space I was in alone, without the distraction of my friend. It was a scary journey and though my support network was strong, I had never felt more alone. I read the book, *Daring Greatly,* by Brene Brown which included a passage that brought me to tears. She included an excerpt from a psychologist about "sliding door moments." Sliding door moments are the small moments that have monumental impact. They are not the moments that everyone can see like coaching your kid's sports teams or helping around the house. They are those quiet moments when you choose to show up, even though something else is calling you (work, a good book, your friends). A sliding door moment can appear in an instant and if missed, the effect is detrimental to building emotional trust. Two incidents were monumental sliding door moments that proved it was time to let go of the life I spent most of my adult years fighting for.

Intimacy had become obligatory and mechanical. My husband's only sign for wanting to have sex was coming into our bedroom and locking the door. That began to irritate me to no end. There was no connection during the day. No playfulness. Hardly any communication. But sex was still expected. One time in particular, we began to go through the motions that our physical relationship had become. Meaning, my body was there, but my heart and spirit were gone. It was obligatory and I was not present emotionally—at all. It appeared to matter little to my husband. He didn't notice the tears I tried to hide. Lying beside him, I cried myself to sleep as he fell into a deep rhythmic snore that drowned out any possibility of him feeling my loneliness.

The next day, I called my aunt and could hardly talk through the tears. I drove to a park and sat in the car and explained how empty the experience left me.

"Why are you having sex if you don't want to?"

I did not know how to answer her simple question. I sat perplexed. I had sex because I believed that was part of the job description. I never considered the thought that not having sex was an option. I was still living the role and doing what was expected of a wife to do, regardless as to what my emotional or physical needs were. I didn't realize or even conceptualize that I had choices. It took me about three months of continuing to do what I was supposed to do until I just couldn't anymore. I went up to NJ to celebrate another aunt's 50th birthday, and on the airplane ride home, decided that I would not have sex with my husband again until he was able to connect with my heart. I wrote him a long detailed text explaining why I had made this decision and what would need to happen to reverse it. I sent it off so he would get it by the time I returned home. In my mind, I thought this will definitely get his attention because physical affection was very important to him. It didn't do what I had hoped. Instead of trying to connect emotionally, he couldn't move beyond the reality that I wasn't budging and sex was out of the question. One morning during his frustration, we started talking. He was complaining about the no sex declaration, and how this was frustrating for him, but did not discuss the lack of connection situation. I couldn't believe that he just didn't get it. He was more concerned with the lack of physical release than to even begin working on what he could do to help us re-connect. After several attempts of trying to explain, I looked at him and asked, "Do you think you could or are even capable of giving me all your heart?" I was sitting on the tub when I asked and he looked at me sincerely and answered, no. "I'm not there...yet." Although I appreciated his honesty, the words cut through my skin like a knife, but I wanted the truth. We had been together for eighteen years, and he was not there...yet. I began crying uncontrollably, and he came over and hugged me. My head was in his chest and I was crying very heavily at this point when his phone rang. It was our neighbor who was waiting for him to workout. He looked at me.

"Go ahead," I said. He left as I sat alone in the middle of my bathroom drowning in my own tears. He left. Yes, I could have said, stay with me and work through this with me, but I wanted him to say, "Hell no, I am not going to leave you like this. I am going to stay right here and fight for you and us." Suddenly, it hit me. I wanted his actions to follow his words, and they did. He could not give me all of his heart, which is why he was able to leave me in my deepest sorrow. His actions followed his words; this was just the first time I acknowledged it. This was not the first sliding door moment that was missed, but I had not allowed myself to see it in the past.

Later that day, or the next, he said, "I kind of feel like maybe I should have stayed."

"Yeah, you should have, but you escaped." We never had sex again.

The next incident that gave me clarity was when my husband approached me to go to counseling. With the bathroom scene still in my mind, I was thinking how could I go to counseling with someone whose heart is not open? I had just returned from being away at a girl's weekend. It was a great weekend and I bonded and shared with one of my sister's close friends. I was scared and lost, and shared where I was with her. She had been through something similar, and looked at me holding my hand and said, "You will know when you are ready." Those words were so empowering. She was right. I had to trust my spirit and trust that only I knew what was right for me and the timing would be revealed when I was ready. I had to trust myself. Those words were one of the best pieces of advice that I got during that part of my journey, and I use those words often with my clients to this day. Prior to leaving for the weekend with the girls, my husband mentioned going to a marriage counselor. I didn't put much thought into it because I'd told him if he really wanted us to go, he needed to set it up. I returned home from the girl's trip in the evening. While I was away, he must have done some work because he handed me a paper with the bios of four different counselors. He had done the research and asked me to review the four he had chosen. I went upstairs and I called my sister and told her about his request. I also told her my spirit didn't trust him. I felt like he just wanted to go because he knew he had to do something. It appeared as though he was just crossing off a checklist item to appear like he was doing something. Her response to me was, "I know you and if your marriage doesn't work out, you will want to believe that you did everything you could to save it." She was right. She did know me, and I would question myself if I did not go to counseling, so I decided I would give him and counseling a chance. When he returned to the room after lying down with my youngest daughter before bedtime he said, "You looked uneasy when I left. Do you want to talk about what is on your mind?"

"You look sleepy; we can talk in the morning."

"No, I want to hear what you want to say."

I thought, wow, this is unlike him; maybe he is really serious about going to counseling.

"Okay, if you insist," and I began to explain my anxiety about going to counseling. Before I finished the first sentence, he fell asleep! I sat in my bed, upright, and stunned.

"You're kidding me, right? You really just fell asleep in the middle of my first sentence?"

He responded, incoherently, "Yeah...." At that point, I still had tears left. I wanted to believe he could be what I needed him to be. I was still on the porch waiting, because the smallest gesture of him saying, "I want to hear what you have to say," gave me hope. It was a hope that was stolen without completing one full sentence. I sat there thinking, if a friend of mine or even an acquaintance of mine needed to talk in the middle of the night, I would put some water on my face and be there for them. That's what I wanted from my life partner. I wanted him to be there for me. I sat there thinking, "If I didn't have those three amazing kids depending on me, I would walk away right now!" That morning he tried to revisit the conversation, but it was too late. I told him I would not go to counseling with him, but he should go for himself. I had already allowed him to fall asleep throughout our marriage similar to how he fell asleep the night before. I did so because I didn't realize I was worth him staying awake. I allowed myself to not matter in our marriage because I didn't believe I mattered in general. This time, I chose me and this was not something he was used to. I had changed, and I was not willing to go through the motions knowing his heart was not fully invested, and now mine wasn't either. That small percentage that I kept for myself was beginning to expand, and no one in my world was prepared for the new person that was emerging.

CHAPTER 16
FINDING THE COURAGE TO BE
HONEST WITH MY KIDS

*"Owning our story can be hard but not nearly as
difficult as spending our lives running from it."*
-Brené Brown

*U*ncovering my truth was one thing, but how on earth could I tell my kids that I was not happy in our picture any longer? It was me that created this magical, "perfect world" for my three beautiful angels. I tried everything in my power to protect them from the dangers of the world, the realities of our world, and I wanted them to see me as the perfect mom. I had no idea the damage I was doing to them or myself by trying to live a façade. For years after my initial epiphany, what kept me paralyzed from moving forward in any real way was preserving the perfect life I'd created for my kids. During this time, usually in the shower, or on one of my runs, I began to pray, and cry, and pray, and cry, and just talk. I began to ask God to show me signs. I would ask God to give me courage. This might sound crazy, but each time I asked, God showed up and I got the sign and courage to move forward. The universe always shows us signs, but we have to be open to receiving them. There are two incidents in particular that occurred with my children that punched me in the gut, and made me look in the mirror and ask the following question. Who were you really protecting Alicia, them or you?

The first situation happened with my oldest child. Our washer and dryer had broken, and I thought this was a perfect opportunity to teach her what it's like to go to a laundromat. After we packed up the car, got some laundry detergent and lots of quarters, our new experience began. Well for anyone who has ever been to a laundromat, after all the clothes are in the washer, and then the dryer, there is really nothing to do but read or talk. My daughter, fifteen at the time, loves to talk. As we began to talk, she began to express some things she and her brother had witnessed regarding me and my husband. She continued to disclose that she and her brother had discovered some disturbing things about their dad. She has a very honest, matter of fact way of communicating. I love her honesty, but she doesn't always realize the effect her words have on people. As she continued to chatter away and describe their feelings toward me, the huge blow to my gut came without warning.

"Mom, we just thought you were kinda weak and clueless." After that blow, everything else she said was a blur. I tried to keep a happy face and get through folding the clothes by nodding and smiling as the endless chatter continued, but I felt like I was having trouble breathing...again. I held it together as we packed up the car to head home. We pulled into the garage and she went into the house and started watching TV. I stopped before going inside. With tears flowing, I texted one of my closest friends, "The dress is getting too small for me to wear anymore." She knew what that meant and offered her love and concern.

I couldn't believe my oldest child could see me in that light. Didn't she see all that I did to protect her and our perfectly constructed world? Didn't she see the amount of strength and sacrifice I needed in order to keep her life intact? Quite simply, no. She didn't see that because kids see through your bullshit. My heart ached after that conversation. It ached because I now realized that both she and her younger brother not only grasped that there were cracks in the foundation, they were hurting, confused, and didn't know how to ask or get the answers they needed from their parents. My heart ached because I also didn't know how or if I had what it took to turn things around. I didn't want my daughter to view me as weak and clueless, but more importantly, I didn't want weak and clueless to ever be an option for her. I also didn't want my son to think it is okay to pretend that everything is okay, when it is not. I had to break the cycle of unworthiness, but how could I teach it, if I wasn't living it? A huge aha moment! It was my daughter that turned the mirror on me and it was my son who finally pushed me out of my paralysis and forced me to face my "stuff."

Several months after the conversation with my daughter, another situation occurred with my son. Remember how I'd prayed to God to give me signs? Well, be careful what you pray for. My son had gotten in trouble for going behind our backs and buying a pair of sneakers after we told him not to. When I realized what he had done, I sent a group text to him and his father. It was a detailed statement regarding losing trust and what that does. My son, clearly remorseful for his actions, also responded to the text with a blow to both of his parents. He first apologized for going behind our backs and was sorry for betraying our trust but didn't feel like we were being fair in our decision to keep him from buying a pair of sneakers with his own money. He then expressed his discomfort, disappointment, and loss of trust in us. Specifically, with a situation of his father's that he had witnessed that had stayed with him for a long time. I was in Walmart picking up items for dinner when the text came through. Once again, the mirror was turned on us and we were forced to recognize that no matter how much we try to hide from the truth, our kids see through it all. That evening, something changed inside of me. I could no longer hide. I could not protect any longer, because after all, I was absolutely failing in that area. My husband and I spoke about the text exchange.

"You need to have an honest conversation with your son. Don't make empty promises you have no intention on keeping or use words that won't be backed with action. This is a pivotal point of your father-son relationship and I pray you don't lose him." I also told him I wanted to say a few things before exiting the room and leaving them to talk. When my son came in, I started the conversation with his punishment for purchasing the sneakers without permission. He accepted it without issue and owned what he had done. Then, I told him we have to address the second part of the text that challenged his trust in us.

I looked my son in the eyes, "I am incredibly proud of the amount of courage it took to hold your dad and I accountable for our actions. You must have looked at that send button a long time before pushing it and that was so brave." He nodded in agreement as tears flowed down his face. "I want to apologize because I knew this was on your heart (remember my daughter had told me at the laundromat), and I never addressed it. I am requiring honesty and trust from you but I'm not doing the same for myself. I didn't protect you and I let you believe that I was okay with it and I am not." His face looked stunned that I would be apologizing to him. He later told me he thought he was going to get a beating. I hugged him tight and said, "I love you with all my heart and you deserve my honesty. The truth is that your dad and I are having serious problems. I'm not okay with any of the things you and your sister have witnessed and I don't know if we are going to be able to work it out. But the one thing that will never change is that we both love you and will be there for you no matter where this path may lead." I continued to hug him tightly while repeatedly stating how proud I was of him. Then, I left and to this day, don't know what transpired between he and his father.

The final sign came a few months later when the kids and I were preparing to go to Florida for spring break. The week leading up to the trip was a tough one. I'd had a breast cancer scare and was on my way to get the results alone (my husband had forgotten that was the day). Normally, I would have reminded him several times, but had entered a period where I wanted to see if he would remember on his own. I confirmed the appointment with him just days before, and I wanted to see if he would be capable of making me a priority in his busy world. He called me on the way to the doctor's office. I thought he remembered but he'd actually called to ask me about something dealing with our finances. I was a little disappointed, but not really. I was becoming numb at this point. The financial issue he called about, which I was also dealing with that same day, was due to a lie he had told me regarding our taxes. This was just one more thing to add to our already growing pile of issues.

Thankfully, I got great news as my biopsy was negative. I was so relieved and truly grateful, and shared the news with my family. In the midst of sharing my good news, I got a call from a parent on my daughter's cheer team that a young cheer mom died from a chronic illness. My emotions on this day were all over the place. I went from happiness and relief, to sadness and regret. That night, I decided to go out to dinner instead of cooking because I had nothing left. I was physically and emotionally drained and still hadn't shared the news of the cheer mom with my daughter. The five of us went to a local restaurant. It was a tough night for all of us, and I shared the news at dinner about the cheer mom. We were all sad and reflective. My husband broke the silence, and began to talk to us all during dinner about a young student who was doing great things in the community. We all kind of looked at him like where is this coming from, but I think that what he was trying to express was that even through adversity, this kid dug deep and is contributing to the world in a big way. He wanted us to support him and the student by attending a scholarship dinner on the coming Saturday. The kids and I were leaving on Sunday for our spring break road trip, but my oldest really wanted to support her dad. Because this is what I always did and because I didn't want to disappoint my daughter, with very short notice, I pulled us all together, and we met him at the dinner. The night was nice, and I felt a sense of pride (still on the porch) as I always did when supporting something he believed in. We looked good and fit the picture perfectly as always. We were about to leave, and my youngest said, "I'll see you at home daddy," and he said, "I'm not coming straight home; I'm going to go out with a few friends." She looked at him perplexed, because didn't he know we were leaving in the morning for a weeklong trip away from him? I wasn't surprised and something in my gut told me he wouldn't make it home that night. Unfortunately, I was right. The one thing that he always regretted, and that was a constant thorn in our marriage was his binge drinking. It was also the one thing I told him would be my deal breaker. And it is the one thing he did over and over again. It wasn't often, but it would always happen as soon as I got secure that it really wouldn't happen again. For so long I wanted his actions to support his words, but I was so blind that I didn't realize they were supporting his words; they just weren't the words that I wanted to hear. This time was different because I was getting braver and closer to being off the porch. I didn't call all over the world to look for him as I had done in the past. In fact, I didn't notice he wasn't home until about 6:30am. I decided to get up and pack the car and be gone before he got home. He called about 8am explaining he drank too much and he was looking for his keys. My response was that we would be gone before he returned, so don't rush. I didn't show any anger or resentment with the kids. We packed the car and set out for our adventure but I knew I would not return the same. My marriage was over. I would not return to the porch again. There were no more chances, and no more room for empty words, with empty actions. My marriage was over, not because of my husband, but because I decided to get off the porch.

When I returned home, I asked my husband to move into the guest room. In my mind, I thought we could co-exist in the same house and be separated while being good parents to our children. He did not want to do it, but I told him if he didn't, I would. Because my husband is a gentleman, he would not let me move, so he moved into the guest room the night we returned. He was sad, lost, and down, and could not muster the energy or desire to penetrate my heart, so he did what was our norm. He waited me out and did nothing.

My husband's decision to stay out drinking all night and miss seeing us off, was the last sign from God that I needed. During that trip, I bonded with my kids like never before. I let them see me and honestly think they like me more for it. My son had a meltdown over something small, so my oldest daughter took it as a chance to connect with him and talk about all that had happened over the past several months. The conversation revealed that my son was blaming himself for the problems in my marriage. He thought that if he had not said something in that text, things would be different. Upon realizing the burden my son was carrying, I made it my mission to continue to communicate with him and assure him that our issues had nothing to do with his message. The problems were present years before, but his courage inspired me to be brave as well. I also made it my mission to be real and vulnerable with them so that they would be real and vulnerable with me. By the end of the trip, my daughter said, "Mom, you are so strong and I really admire you." Those words were like hitting the lottery and as unsure the road ahead of me appeared, it didn't matter because I never want my children to view me as weak and clueless again. Strong, imperfect, and real are what I would want them to remember me as; and if I die tomorrow, I know I changed the legacy I will leave behind. I am good with that!

CHAPTER 17
BEING UNCOMFORTABLE FUELS CHANGE

"I WILL BEAT HER. I will train harder. I will eat cleaner. I know her weakness. I know her strengths. I've lost to her before, but not this time. She is going down. I have the advantage because I know her well. She is the Old Me."

-Bonnie Pfiester

*B*eing separated while still living in the same house was increasingly more uncomfortable with each passing day. I had been honest with my kids on where we were and what was happening but my husband was still in denial. He was expressing a different reality. It was his reality but he had still not realized how much I had changed. I honestly believe, though separated, he thought that I would get over my feelings and things would go back to normal. He was waiting me out and because he was dealing with his own grief and denial, that is all he did. He was depressed and unresponsive and the mood in the house was heavy. It was beginning to affect his relationship with the kids. Because I was being so honest with them, they began to be honest as well. When he would ask them about how they felt, they were honest and told him that they felt we were better apart. This hurt him and the depression grew. By now, the kids were out of school and my plan was to go to Florida to stay with my sister for most of the summer. It was a chance to get away, be surrounded by love and support, and develop my plan for the future. Because I can work remotely, it was a non-issue for my job. I'd decided to leave right after Father's Day. My husband was against it but I didn't give much of a choice. For Father's Day in the past, we usually attended an alumni breakfast that honored fathers. This year, my husband was selected to speak. He had also invited some close friends to attend. Because I had not figured out what was appropriate in our in-home separation and what was not, I agreed to attend with the kids. At the breakfast, I felt very uncomfortable because on the outside, it appeared nothing had changed. When it was his turn to speak, he gave a moving tribute to each one of us. He expressed what we've been for him and credited us for his ability to speak to the group that Sunday. Although it was beautiful and heartfelt, it put me on the spot because while I believed his words were sincere, the reality of where we were at that time was gravely different.

After the breakfast, we came home and I went to my room to lie down. He came upstairs and laid on my bed and began to rub my ankle.

"I am trying to connect with you but you seem closed down."

Honestly, I was stunned. Closed down, really? We are separated. We've had no emotional or physical connection in months and we barely talk. Why would I behave differently? His question frustrated me to no end.

Later that evening, I cooked dinner and we all watched the NBA finals. At some point, I received a phone call and went up to my room. My oldest daughter had a fit and came to me angry, questioning why I would take the call during "family time." I ended my call and asked her to come to my room. I wanted to understand what was really going on. She started crying and said it felt like we were a family again, and I had left. I let her express her feelings before empathetically telling her that although I understood, our family was different now. We got to a good space, but I was far from good. I felt STUCK.

I went to bed that night with a heavy heart. The next day, my husband called from work and we had a long conversation. His words validated my initial feeling. He was waiting me out. Waiting for this to pass. Waiting for me to pop back into who I was and make everything alright. I hung up the phone, got in my car, and drove to a nearby park. I sat in the parking lot and cried, and cried, and cried. I didn't call anyone. I needed to be alone. After about forty-five minutes of uncontrollable tears, I looked in the mirror, and realized the only person keeping me stuck was me. The words, "you will know when you are ready," came rushing back. I knew what had to happen before I returned from my summer in Florida. I had written a letter explaining that I wanted an official separation with separate living spaces. I decided I would mail it to him after my son joined us in Florida (he was coming a week later). During our drive down to Florida, my husband called and expressed how hard it was to see us leave. "But you expressed nothing and did nothing to stop us." My comment pushed the conversation forward and I told him about the letter. This was probably not the best thing, since my son was still with him, and this pushed him further into a dark and depressed state. He did not want to accept that our marriage was over and seemed to be spiraling. Once I got to Florida, I had to figure out a plan to financially and physically make this happen. It was extremely tough and would take great sacrifice. My husband fought it a bit and things got a little ugly, but in the end, he agreed to leave the house.

My husband was in a dark place, and needed something to blame for our separation. As he began to share the news that I wanted a separation, he also shared my indiscretion. It was peculiar because in all the time that had passed since discovering my betrayal, we never discussed it again after that dinner date. It really came as a surprise as people began to call me and reveal that he was sharing this information. I guess at that time it was easier to look outside of himself to explain how this could have happened. What he didn't know was that I had already shared my entire truth with the people that mattered to me. They knew our marriage ending had little to do with the other person and solely to do with the changes I had made in myself. So, as my husband spiraled, I decided to remain positive and grounded in my truth. I made a promise to myself that our ending would not be negative. No matter what!

During that summer, I told him that while I couldn't wrap my head around how negative he had gotten, regardless of what he said or did, I would not reciprocate. Because his nature is not ugly and malicious, it did not last long. What he had said and done were out of pain and a broken heart. I knew it and had faith that he would come around, which he did. Though he struggled for years, the actual negativity lasted maybe three weeks. We never wanted to hurt each other and thankfully, that became the focus. My husband was always a good provider and always gave me a sense of security that he would always be there. Honestly, I believe he would still be there, but just being there wasn't enough for me any longer. Even though he did not agree, he produced an official separation agreement that we both signed, and he committed to be financially supportive, so the kids and I could remain in our home. Neither of us wanted to disrupt their lives more than absolutely required. He remains a great provider and through his own growth journey, has stepped into being a great co-parent.

CHAPTER 18
SEEKING VALIDATION

"If you live for people's acceptance, you will die from their rejection."

-Lecrae

*M*y new life off the porch began in July of 2014. As I packed my car and prepared to say my goodbyes to my sister and aunt, my heart was heavy. They were my safety net, my sounding board, and the greatest support through it all. They took special care of me over the five weeks of my refuge and as I made the hardest decision of my adult life. I felt loved. I felt secure. Now I was packing my three kids up to head back to a life that was no more. It was a new beginning and such a sorrowful ending all at the same time. I was scared! I was terrified actually! Yet, I also felt strong and ready to face my new reality. There was no turning back now and it was time to go back home and figure things out on my own. I was not a scared little girl anymore. I was becoming a strong, powerful, brave, courageous woman and mother and I was going to continue to show my kids that honesty, truth, courage, and strength are what I'm fighting for: for them and me.

Several weeks after we separated, my husband came over on a Tuesday night to see the kids. It was important for him to spend time with the kids without me being there, so I took the opportunity to get in some "me time." I got a pedicure and took myself to the movies to see *The Hundred-Foot Journey*. It was a really sweet movie about the journey of life, and of course I started thinking about my journey. I was overcome with emotion and felt like I needed to share my thoughts with my husband. Though I felt the timing was perfect, it apparently was not. I wrote:

"So many times over the last 3 years I've wanted you to fight. I wanted you to do whatever necessary to get me back. I wanted you to dig deep in your soul and show me that I was enough. I realize now that you couldn't do that. For whatever reason, you were just not capable of doing it. Maybe it was me or maybe it was you, but I finally decided I was enough to fight for, and I've started to live. Each day that passes brings new challenges, and I feel like I'm on this incredible journey by myself. I didn't know if I would survive if you didn't fight, but I did. I'm learning to be okay with being alone with myself. Very lonely sometimes, but I'm finding my way.

I'm not looking for anyone to save me...a first. Since the devastating rejection of my father year after year, I was waiting and waiting for someone to save me. I thought you were that person, and when you couldn't, I was devastated.

But I've learned to really accept life as a journey. And for a very long time, you provided a place of security and safety for me. When that safety was gone, I was forced to find my own way. My own security. This has been a blessing for me. I found real love...real love for myself. I'm learning to take care of my heart and that's something I didn't know I was capable of doing. I'm taking one day at a time, and I'm living and learning on my own terms.

I will always love you and what we created, and I pray you learn to love yourself as much as others love you. I know you view our "ending" as a failure, but maybe it's the beginning for you as well.

I don't want you to respond. These are some thoughts and feelings I needed to release."

Well, he did respond, and proved my timing was awful. He was blinded by his own pain and was wallowing in self-pity. The wounds were still wide open and I should have had better judgment. I set myself up for disappointment and fueled his anger and resentment. In his eyes, he did fight, and he was just doing what I requested. He pretty much said, "If you want me back, I'll come back tomorrow. If not, leave it alone." So, I left it alone and never sought validation from him again. About six months later, he gave me a very beautiful Valentine's Day Card. Unsolicited, he acknowledged playing the victim and expressed that he didn't look at things from my perspective. He said he never considered how difficult it must have been to make the choices I had made. That card brought tears to my eyes. It was not an expensive gift but his words meant more to me than anyone could imagine. Actually, they meant more to me than they should have.

The next day, I sent him a text saying how much his words meant. Within thirty seconds, the validation I yearned for and received was snatched away. He replied, "You're welcome, but I still don't agree with the separation..." I felt immediately deflated. How could he not agree with the separation if he really understood how difficult my choices were? If he understood how profound our disconnect was? Initially, I was disappointed but the lesson I learned in both interactions was that validation from others (especially those closest to you) is important and feels good, but as easily as it is given, it can be taken away. Real validation has to come from within. It comes from that inner voice that I have come to trust and rely on. It is mine and cannot be taken away as long as I continue to trust myself, my voice, and my spirit.

CHAPTER 19
LEARNING TO LIVE OFF THE PORCH

"Authenticity is a collection of choices that we have to make every day. It's about the choice to show up and be real. The choice to be honest. The choice to let our true selves be seen."

-Brené Brown

The first several months of our separation were very difficult. We were adjusting and establishing new norms. We had to figure out how visitation would work. Should I stay at the house or leave when he visited? Since he didn't have a living space conducive for kids, should he stay at the house on weekends? Do we talk? We were in unchartered territory, and my husband was full of resentment towards me. I could feel it in every encounter, though he communicated with me very little. It seemed, he wanted me to fail. He wanted me to see how hard it would be without having him there. The more I learned to do things on my own, the more he resented me. He didn't talk to me. He seemed angry or edgy all the time, and he would make comments to the kids that made them very uncomfortable. At times, we wouldn't hear from him for weeks, and then he would be there—still angry, still resentful, and very sad. This time was uncomfortable for all of us.

Finally, the silence was broken and we had to discuss a more permanent solution to his living arrangement. We decided to talk and the conversation went on for hours. He started by saying he didn't want to give up on us and that he wanted us to fight. I was actually stunned. He had not spoken to me for about four months outside of the kid's needs and now he was telling me he wanted to fight for us. I remained calm as he spoke. I prayed to God to help me stay honest and true to myself. When he was done, I carefully told him that I did not want to fight and that over the past four months, I hadn't seen one sign that told me that I had made the wrong decision. If anything, my decision was validated by some of his actions which had been the catalyst for us arriving at the separation in the first place. Then I asked what exactly was he angry about? As we pulled back the layers, he revealed that he was mostly angry with himself. I also believe he was angry with me for getting off the porch. Regardless, I knew there was no fighting or going back. He still didn't see me, he just saw the life he had, and wanted it back. I can't blame him. It was a life where he didn't have to do much to maintain the relationships. I did it all. Now, he was faced with having to make an effort to connect with our kids. He could no longer depend on my connection with them. He had to develop it for himself, and not only with our kids, but all the relationships in his life. He had to invest himself and this is what he most resisted. At this time, he was filled with too much resentment but he would eventually be grateful for his connection with our kids, which was birthed because I got off the porch. My being on the porch for so long not only affected the quality of my life, but everyone else that meant the world to me. Once I broke free, it inspired others to do the same.

CHAPTER 20
TAKING OFF MY WEDDING RINGS

"Nothing ever goes away until it teaches us what we need to know."
-Pema Chodron

*E*ven though we were separated, I still wore my wedding bands for quite a while. For no reason other than I couldn't imagine not wearing them. One Saturday, my husband said he was coming to spend time with the kids. Again, I took this as an opportunity to get some alone time in. While I was out, my oldest daughter didn't complete the chores I had required before her going out, so I was very upset. She was at a friend's house, so I went and picked her up and told her to get in her room and complete the tasks I'd given her. Meanwhile, as I was updating my husband on what the tasks were that my daughter was to complete, he informed me that he was going to a friend's house to see the fight. I looked at him puzzled because I thought his purpose for being there was to spend time with the kids. I rolled my eyes and left.

The frustration built in my spirit. He texted and told me the kids were "covered" and they were all with friends and he would be going to the fight at 10pm. "Since you are not with the kids, you might as well go on home."

"I'm not going there with you," he stated dismissively.

I was furious because I felt like he was playing games. I stayed out until after 10pm and when I returned, he was gone. However, his car was still at the house. I went to bed early taking advantage of an empty house. At about 5:30 am I was awakened by the door chime. Yes, not only did he not spend time with the kids, but he went out, pictures of his wild night were posted on Facebook, and he returned to my home at 5:30am. For our entire marriage, we battled with him binge drinking one to two times a year. He would stay out drinking, not call, and return home at the crack of dawn. This was something we argued about and something that hurt me time and time again. Now, for him to do it while we were separated (a separation he did not want), and completely disrespect me and the peace I had discovered, was really the smack in the face I needed.

Later that morning, I went for a run, went grocery shopping, and called Clean to tell him what had transpired. I asked if I was being unreasonable? Though I knew I wasn't, he validated my feelings. After I finished my errands, I went home and told him to get up and get out. I told him how disrespected I felt and that he needed to go since there were no kids in sight for him to spend time with. After he left, I took a lot of big breaths. I felt pretty proud of myself for requiring him to leave. Alicia on the porch would have felt helpless, and just waited for him to wake up at his leisure. I was like, wow look at you girl! The morning was potentially going downhill. I had plans to go to a salsa lesson with a friend who cancelled on me, and my spirit was still quite upset. I went upstairs, looked in the mirror, and I said NO! You are going to your salsa class by yourself and you got the sign you needed to take those rings off. *He is who he is and he is not going to change, but you have.*

I took my rings off but still didn't have the courage to show him that I'd removed them. Whenever he came to visit, I would put them back on. I went to a family party and my aunt noticed I'd taken my rings off but I told her I put them back on when he is around. She looked at me and the look was all I needed. It took a couple of weeks, but her look struck me to the core. How can I say I am living authentically when I am still hiding? Around this time is when I decided to become a life coach. The first requirement for my coaching certification program was to attend a weekend coaching certification training. During this training, I was coached on why I was continuing to put the rings on in my husband's presence. The answer became crystal clear. I was still protecting him, his feelings, and his image, by dishonoring my own truth. After that weekend, I decided that I would name my coaching practice, *Getting Off the Porch*, and would live my truth. I would not hide anymore. How could I be a great coach if I wasn't living my brand and my truth?

It was during that long conversation when he said he wanted to fight for us, that I reminded him of this night. I told him I took my rings off and why. He did not and could not say a thing, because I would not hide behind his actions or lack thereof and neither could he. Though we are not divorced, it was at this point that I began to acknowledge that he was no longer my husband, so from this point on I will refer to him as my ex-husband.

Although my rings were off, it was weird not having a ring on that finger after eighteen years, so I bought myself a new ring. It was a sterling silver ring that said faith. When I put it on, I married myself. I looked at it several times throughout the day and it was a constant reminder of the level of faith required for me to stay and live off the porch.

CHAPTER 21
CLEANING OUT THE GARAGE

"Faith is taking one step even when you don't see the whole staircase."
-Martin Luther King

*A*bout six months into the separation, my garage began to cause me great discomfort. I would drive home every day and feel overwhelmed by the amount of "stuff" filling the space. Some days it would cause me physical anxiety. I would pull into the garage and sit for a few minutes in my car. As I would look around at the disorganization and clutter, I felt weighed down and overwhelmed. I wondered why it caused such discomfort; after all, it was my "stuff" right? I still hadn't made the connection at the time, but I believe the "stuff" in that garage represented the "stuff" that I had to deal with in my life. The more I didn't deal with "my inner stuff," the more uncomfortable I got each time I pulled into that garage. I could not escape the "stuff!" My marriage was ending and though I was clear that it was the right choice, the road ahead was still uncertain. The "stuff" continued to remind me of the huge mountain that was ahead of me/us.

Though it was noble of my ex-husband to move out so that the kids and I could maintain our lifestyle, it was hard as hell. Our home was still our home, and all of the memories in the home were staring at me each and every day. The good memories, which there were a lot of, were a constant reminder of all that I chose to give up. Though my life began to change drastically, my external space did not change at all. My living space began to feel increasingly awkward. I even began thinking about selling the house and moving so that I could really have a fresh start. This however, would have been an emotional choice, not a sound economic choice. With the housing economy still not where it was when we purchased our home, selling it would not yield a meaningful profit. Moving was not an option. I've noticed patterns in my life and I don't like feeling uncomfortable, especially in my home. For me, discomfort always leads to action. Since the Christmas break was fast approaching, I decided that my bedroom needed a complete overhaul. Every time I walked into my bedroom, it brought back memories of the life I had with my husband. There was a tribute on the wall with pictures of our life together, and wall art that talked about our commitment. It hurt profoundly to be reminded each day of how far away that life was. The hurt ran deep because when I did the mural, I was completely invested in the pictures that were so a part of who I thought I was. As I stood and stared at the tribute on the wall, with tears streaming I decided to rip the bandage off and do something to change my living space. To be honest, that was much easier than tackling the garage. My big sister spent the holidays with us. She knew the first holiday season separated would be difficult. Her gift to me was to help redecorate my room. The first weekend, my ex-husband decided to take the kids away from the home was the perfect time to pull it all off. I was a little anxious to be alone for the first time without the kids, so filling that space with something exciting was good. I am the hand-me-down queen of the family and my sister had just redecorated her room, so I asked if I could have her old comforter set, which was fabulous. It had all of the throw pillows, drapes, and even a matching mirror for above the bed. That Friday night, after I received the items from my sister, I headed to Home Depot. I picked out the paint and headed home to get the room prepped. I decided to turn the tribute wall into an accent wall. As I began to paint over the words, "Grow old with me, the best is yet to be" sadness filled my heart. Tears fell as the words disappeared with each stroke. It was a sad and lonely night, but it was so necessary.

I woke the next morning drained from the emotion, yet somewhat relieved and proud of myself for allowing the feeling to flow, but not letting them stop me from moving forward. My sister arrived about a week later. She added a keen sense of design to the room with her finishing touches, and my bedroom was now a tranquil sanctuary of peace. It was now filled with positive affirmations, beautiful earthy colors, and pictures of my kids and my support network. I wake up each day surrounded by my "why" and it feels like a big hug.

Going into the New Year, after my sister and nephew left, I felt better and stronger. However, I still had to pull into that garage each day and that "stuff" continued to stare at me. I would try to look down and go straight to my tranquil bedroom, but it didn't work. I continued to have this heavy feeling as soon as the garage door went up. It became too uncomfortable to ignore. Finally, I had a day off of work around February of that year and decided that would be the day I would clean out the garage! I had a cup of coffee, put on my work clothes, and walked into the (large, three car) garage to start cleaning it out from one end to the other. Before I knew it, there was a huge garbage pile, and next to that was two huge thrift store donation piles, and next to that was three gigantic bags to donate to Goodwill. About five hours later, not only was the garage clean and organized, but so was the storage shed that is attached to my home. I stood in the garage alone when I was done, and was tickled pink with myself. I looked something that seemed bigger than me in the face, and tackled it! ON MY OWN! I realized I could do anything I put my mind to, but I also acknowledged that you can't do anything until you are mentally, physically, and emotionally ready to do so.

CHAPTER 22
RECOVERY IS ON GOING

"Recovery is the bridge between who you were and who you choose to be."

-Anonymous

I started 2015 strong, clear, focused, and ready to be, live, and grow off the porch. I redecorated my bedroom, cleaned out my garage, and changed my own license plates on my car (big for me). March came, and about mid-way through, I fell flat on my butt! One night I went to print something, and the printer cord was missing. I asked each kid where it was and they all said, "I don't know." I lost it! Like "wire hanger" lost it like in the movie *Mommy Dearest.* All three of them looked at me like I was crazy and my daughter said something disrespectful under her breath. I stormed upstairs and got in my bed and cried. I fell apart. I didn't get out of bed all week. By that Friday, I was falling fast in a downward spiral. I had signed up to go to a workshop several months earlier, and the reminder popped up on my calendar. The workshop was called, "Get Unstuck, Be Unstoppable." I had bought the book early, and the workshop was a bonus. I actually thought about not going, but something in my spirit was saying you need to go to this workshop. I was falling into a depression, and actually prayed that the workshop would do "something" to bring me out of my funk. There were over 100 people at the workshop, and the energy alone was beginning to lift my spirit. As the workshop began, I was exceedingly open to receiving a message or breakthrough. I needed something specifically for me. About halfway through, it happened. Valorie Burton, the book's author and the woman leading the workshop, said something that completely hit home for me.

"Sometimes we let go of control or things that keep us stuck in some areas of our lives, and then re-focus that control somewhere else."

BAM! It hit me. My journey off the porch led me to make some monumental changes in my life. I'd done an amazing job at letting go of the things that kept me stuck like perfectionism and overcompensating, but without realizing it, I refocused that energy on being a perfect parent in an imperfect situation overcompensating so I would have perfectly happy, well-adjusted children through our HUGE transition. Crazy right? But that is exactly what I was doing. No wonder why I crashed and burned. Because I was the one that caused so much change, I thought it was my responsibility, and that it was in my power and control to make sure that my children adjusted perfectly...NOT!

I took pride in this, because though I had accepted imperfection for myself (or so I thought), I did not accept it in regard to my children. So, when that printer cord went missing, and my daughter spoke to me in a disrespectful tone, and my son made a passive aggressive comment to me the next morning; I fell apart. My heart ached. I was failing and my kids were not adjusting perfectly. I began to doubt myself and all of the decisions I had made.

It was in the middle of that workshop that it clicked. The first sign that I was not in control of my children or how perfectly I had chosen to parent them through this transition, I fell apart at the seams. I decided that I didn't want to be stuck in familiar patterns of "perfectionism," "settling," or "unrealistic expectations" for myself or with my children, so I needed to do something. The first step was to deal with my kids. I woke them up the next morning. It was an unseasonably nice day, and I took them to climb Stone Mountain. As we reached the top, we all sat together, and I had a heart to heart with all three of them! I told them about my breakthrough. I told them that disrespect in any form is unacceptable in our family from them or me. I then apologized for trying to be perfect in an imperfect situation. Finally, I thanked them for loving me through all of my imperfection. I also gave them the space to express whatever was on their mind. We all left Stone Mountain a little lighter.

This journey off the porch and how it affected my kids was very powerful. I've chosen honesty to get through the ups and downs of separation, and I know it works. I continuously ask my kids if they are okay with the changes we've made, and they consistently say they are happier with how things are now as opposed to before. They saw that their parents were not happy, and they see there is more opportunity for happiness apart than together. Still hard to believe that they see things so clearly, but that's what honesty does. It provides clarity. The bottom line for our kids, and most kids, is that they want their parents to be happy and that starts with honesty and courage to be authentic with them.

CHAPTER 23
GETTING OFF THE PORCH AGAIN!

"There are two primary choices in life: to accept conditions as they exist, or accept the responsibility for changing them."
-Denis Waitle

Getting off the porch is a journey, not a destination. Sometimes you wind up back on the porch because there is still something you are hiding from or scared to face.

Months turned into years, and our separation became our new normal. I began navigating what being single looked like and what being alone felt like. I didn't like it! It was terrifying and uncomfortable, and at times very lonely. I entertained a few calls from male admirers, and even went on a few dates, but nothing really transpired. My male friend resurfaced and though I knew it was not healthy to go down that road again, I did because I wanted to feel better. My marriage was over, and the space in my heart seemed vast. The voices of the past began to fill my head. So again, like with my dad, and with my ex-husband, I made myself smaller so that I didn't feel abandoned and alone. I convinced myself that I could just have a casual relationship with no strings attached. I convinced myself that would be enough for me. Just like with my dad, the smallest bit of attention made me feel special. My husband "being there" made me feel secure. My friend's attentiveness made me feel loved.   I was still looking for wholeness outside of myself. It hit me like a ton of bricks. I had not gotten off the porch completely, because I had not looked within to find the missing pieces.   Love, security, and acceptance dwelled in me, but I had not made the connection. So instead of doing what was "right," I gave into feeling better in the now. As much as I tried to enjoy the friendship, it became uncomfortable. The dress was beginning not to fit again. It didn't fit because I was different now, but was still holding on to that little girl on the porch just in case I needed her. I knew I had to break this pattern completely if I was ever going to be free and enough. As I became aware of what I was really doing, I began to grow out of the need to fill the gaps. I wanted to fill my own gaps. As long as I let him be in this space, I would be living a lie and being a fake. The time was now, and there was no turning back.

I finally got the clarity and the courage I need to end it completely. I knew without any doubt that not only was it the right thing to do, it was the only choice for me. The only person that could finally fight for me, was me. The light bulb finally came on!

I was ready but I had a lot of residual feelings for the choices I'd made and they were keeping me trapped in shame and regret. Both shame and regret are worthless feelings. I had to forgive myself in order to move forward. I replaced guilt with gratitude and replaced shame with humility. Had this not happened, and had I not realized how human I could be, I would not be the coach that I am for my clients. Prior to all of my experiences on my Getting Off the Porch journey, I was a judgmental, self-righteous, insecure person. I've released who I was and now walk fully in who I choose to be: powerful, compassionate, and humble. I am now walking fully in my big life with no limits. No more playing it small out of fear. Since making the choice to get off the porch again, opportunities have opened up that at one time were unimaginable. What became increasingly clear was that nothing I was trying to do was going to flourish until I faced my truth and walked fully in it.

CHAPTER 24
FALLING IN LOVE

"To love oneself is the beginning of a lifelong romance."

-Oscar Wilde

I've become obsessed with the concept of falling in love with myself now that I've accepted myself in all of my imperfection. We often complain about how we are treated. How others take advantage of us. How we are not heard. However, I believe generally people treat you the way you treat yourself. For many years, I put myself at the bottom of the priority list. I put my kid's needs and wants before my own. I supported and listened to my ex-husband's dreams and ignored my own. I supported friends and family in ways that compromised my spiritual health. I wasn't very kind to myself but was disappointed when others didn't come through for me in ways I yearned for. How would they know based on how I treated myself? My relationship pattern began with my father, then my husband, and then my indiscretion. I went from one co-dependent relationship to the next. I attracted broken men (like my father) and depended on all of them to fill the layers of pain that I was unable to release. The relationships could never be whole and healthy, because I was broken inside. I was living with the hurt and pain of being abandoned on that porch and that was what I began to attract in my relationships. When I decided to release all that was holding me back from living a full authentic life, I made a commitment to me! I decided that I was going to fall in love with me because I'm worth it! I am cool, compassionate, passionate, fun, quirky, adventurous, and totally over the top! I actually enjoy my company. and I am learning and growing into myself each day. I never took the time to be with me before. Why? Because it was safer to hide behind my secure relationships and everyone else's needs rather than explore my own. What I have found is balance. I still love being a support for my loved ones, but there are quite a few people that are now my village of support because I've given them the chance to show up. I'm learning to fly. I'm learning to take risks. I'm learning to put myself first and put myself out there. I'm learning to be okay with making mistakes and owning them. It's okay to be wrong. I'm learning to be comfortable in stillness. I'm learning that alone time is precious and the perfect opportunity to love, learn, and grow from the inside out. I'm learning that being vulnerable allows others to be there for you. I'm learning that people see me and want to know me now that I like and know myself. I'm embracing my power, and I am more courageous than I ever thought I could be.

Recently I attended a transformational coaching workshop, and as much work as I've done to get off the porch, I continue to realize that the work is never ending, and that it is a journey and not a destination. The facilitator told me, I get it intellectually, but that my heart and mind had not yet connected. She said I needed to find my humanity. *That's deep.* How the hell do I do that? Well, I signed up for the next level of this transformational coaching series and it happened. I discovered I had to let go of those things that kept me on the porch—insecurity, unworthiness, and making myself smaller for others. Yes, I had done the work but had I really let those things go or was I keeping them in a little compartment that I could retreat to if needed? We went through a journey as a group, and I discovered I was still holding on to pieces of that little girl on the porch...just in case. I realized it was time to allow that little girl to disappear completely. She served me well, but was still keeping me trapped in doubt and insecurity. I cried for that little girl, as she drifted away from me. In fact, it was through this journey that I was able to begin writing again. I had written half of my book but could not write another word for years. I was still listening to old voices and following old patterns that just didn't fit this big life I desired for myself.

Through this workshop I discovered that I am no longer an insecure, unworthy, invisible girl. I declared and embrace every day that I am now an assertive, powerful, and empowering leader. I made the choice to be different. Those old thoughts sometimes come back but I shut them down and keep on pushing.

Because this transformational coaching series opened so much for me, I decided to invite my ex-husband and daughter to the pay-it-forward night. I did this because whether we are together or apart as a couple doesn't matter. I want my family to be healed, and I want the cycles of dysfunction to be broken. The only way for that to happen is for us all to do the work. They both signed up for the series and have begun their own journey of healing. By getting the courage to face my biggest fears, I set an example to inspire the most important people in my life to do the work for themselves. Inviting my ex-husband to the workshop was not to bring us back together. It was to help all of us be whole, so that we can live full, healthy, authentic, joyous lives.

A huge discovery for my ex-husband was that we are both completely different, with different communication levels and needs. Soon after he finished the second level of training, he came over to the house and shared a monumental breakthrough he had. I thought wow! Now we can have some real conversations about everything. Now we can get some real closure and I jumped in the deep end of communicating this all to him. This is something I later found out in our marriage caused him to shut down. This is where being over the top is not such a good thing. Again, I crashed and burned. This wasn't about me or us. It was only about him and him finding his way to being happy from the inside out. He gently explained to me the next day that one of the most beautiful things about me is how I communicate. He said I communicate on a level 10 all the time. What he had discovered is that he is a level 2 communicator and he was not ready to communicate with me in the way that I had yearned. I hung up the phone in tears and it took me a couple of months to process and let go of what I thought I needed. I thought I needed this huge conversation where we discussed all that happened, all that went wrong, and all our regrets in order to move forward and really heal. I realized that I really don't need that anymore. I let him know this in the following text:

"After your transformational experience I really went into an emotional roller coaster about us and thought we would have this major conversation about the past, our mistakes, and finally have closure and healing.

However, over the last several months, I realized I don't need that conversation as much as I thought. Last night, I realized through your short but deep statements that we both know clearly where we went wrong. We both know clearly what we gave up. We both invested so much in the cherry on top of our beautiful dessert, that the inside disappeared and fell apart. And we both lost ourselves...for different reasons, but we did.

In finding myself, I had to allow myself to fail, fall, fuck up, and I needed to know I could fight for myself, and that I was worth it. It was hard, terrifying, but I found my light again...and it seems as though you have found your own as well.

You once said you don't think you could be my friend but I hope you were wrong. We aren't the same people we once were but the core of who we are has always been good and beautiful."

His response was short, sweet, and all that I needed.

"Receive all that you said and look forward to being a part of what God intended us to be."

I believe this discovery has gotten us closer to a space of acceptance and healing, because we've accepted that our needs are completely different, and probably always have been. There is no longer an expectation of what the other should or should not be. This has made co-parenting and our friendship possible, authentic, and natural. In living your life authentically, you give others permission to do the same.

CHAPTER 25
LIFE BEYOND THE PORCH

*"I didn't find out who I was, until I found out who
I wasn't."*
                              -Paul Carrick Brunson

I am a completely different person than I was on the porch. In fact, when I tell my story to new people, it is hard for them to imagine that I was okay with being invisible. What is really amazing is that even if I wanted to go back to the porch, I can't. My spirit won't allow it. Sure, there have been times along the way when I've thought, "Alicia, just suck it up." It would be financially easier for everyone involved and things would look a lot neater. But physically, I couldn't fathom that as an option for so many reasons. Mostly because I don't fit anymore and the pain of squeezing into a space way too small for me is scarier than trying to navigate this new world without limits. Aside from myself, my intention is to leave a new legacy for my children. One that gives them permission to be who they are and live fully in their truth. If I've given them anything, it is that freedom to be who they are. I was trying to teach them that concept, but wasn't doing it myself. Now that I am walking fully in my truth, I know I've earned their respect, and it feels amazing!

Initially when I began this journey, a myriad of questions flooded my thoughts.

How will I be able to financially support myself?
Should I move or try to manage this big house alone? Should I change jobs?
Is Atlanta really the place for me now that my world has changed so much?
Do I want to date again?
Will I fall in love again?
Will I ever have my heart and soul made love to again?
Will I finish my book?
Will my new business take off?

And the scariest question of all...am I really enough? The answer is NOW yes, I am enough! Now I have the courage to ask myself those hard questions, and I have the faith to know that my life is unfolding exactly how it is intended to. I trust that the answers will come when I am ready for them. I still have bad days. However, those days that I couldn't get out of bed, don't exist anymore. I've allowed myself to acknowledge and accept that this is a new space and I am going to stumble and fall, but that is part of living beyond the porch. When you are on the porch, you don't get a chance to fall, or get lost, because you are too afraid to move. I am moving, and I am expanding, but I am also stumbling and falling. The great thing about being off the porch is that even when you find yourself on the porch again, you can regroup and get off again and again.

It is liberating!

About halfway through writing this book, I started reading about the power of setting intentions, so I set four intentions:

1. Leave my current job and walk fully in my career as a coach.
2. Find healing and closure with my husband.
3. Walk away from my inappropriate relationship completely.
4. Finish and publish my book.

Though I had no idea how any of them would come to be, they all did! I don't believe they would have ever materialized had I not put them on paper and out in the universe. I also took action, no matter how small or big. Recently, I decided to put a new intention out there for love. My new love intention is: "A man that has done some real work on himself, is honest, and is as invested in me as I am in him. He is funny, sexually compatible, fit, spontaneous, and adventurous...oh, and unmarried and straight."

Regardless of how the universe responds, I know without a doubt that I am enough—with the right someone or standing alone.

REFLECTIONS OFF THE PORCH

*B*efore going to print, I allowed my ex-husband to read the book. I was filled with anxiety. I wrote a fair rendition of my story, but it is raw and honest, and painful to relive.

Although his initial reaction was tough, it pushed us to have a conversation that was long overdue. As we discussed the story, we were both filled with remorse for some of the things we did. But more importantly, we were happy that we both choose to be different today.

Going through the editing process, I connected even more dots. Though my husband and I looked amazing on the outside, we came together looking for the other to fill our brokenness. Though we had no idea at the time, we started off with the odds against us.

For me, the abandonment of my father left me emotionally needy and controlling. I went from one co-dependent relationship to the next so that I didn't have to face the real issues of insecurity and unworthiness.

During the editing process, my publisher posed several questions that caused reflection. What was the *real* deal breaker? Was it the cheating? The drinking? The lying? I told her that's an interesting question because I could have forgiven it all. I would have given up all the things that made a good husband (provider, coach, help around the house) to have his heart and honesty. I could not live without connection or the desire to be better. I wanted a partner. I wanted us to do the work to find our own wholeness and healing. Since he was resistant to doing that, I did it on my own. But what I later realized was that what I needed most was to find my own heart instead of looking to him to make me happy. I found what I needed to be happy. That is priceless.

I've learned to accept that my journey has unfolded exactly the way it should have. The universe tried to get my attention year after year and I ignored all the signs out of fear. I'm so glad I picked up that cell phone. I'm so glad that he cheated. I lost him long before those text messages, and more importantly I realized I never really found myself. The cheating was the big thing that pushed me to find the answers.

Had that big, horrible thing not happened, we would both still be stuck in complacency and obligation. Since our separation, I decided to rewrite the script and leave the porch behind. Though I drove him crazy, pushed him out of his comfort zone time and time again, he is also letting go of the pain of his past and choosing to be better for himself and for our children.

We've created a new picture that welcomes imperfection and respects differences. I recently told him though the process of reviewing the book was painful, we are teaching our kids that standing in your truth no matter how hard it is, has set us free to live our best, authentic lives.

ALICIA'S QUOTES TO LIVE BY

"You can't be brave if you've only had wonderful things happen to you."
-Mary Tyler Moore

"My love is unconditional. My trust and respect are not."
-Anonymous

"The first step off the porch is realizing how you got there in the first place."
-Alicia Booker

"There are two ways of spreading light: to be the candle or the mirror that reflects it."
-Edith Wharton

"Hope is being able to see that there is light despite all of the darkness."
-Desmond Tutu

"Friendship is born at that moment when one person says to another: What! You too? I thought I was the only one."
-C.S. Lewis

"A real love story is sometimes exhausting. A romance is deliberately constructed to yield a certain result; the ambiguities are trimmed out, so it's neater and more pleasing to our hearts. But you don't live a love story, you live a life."
-Melissa Pritchard

"We must let go of the life we have planned, so as to accept the one that is waiting for us."
-Joseph Campbell

"Sometimes you find yourself in the middle of nowhere, and sometimes in the middle of nowhere you find yourself."
-Anonymous

"Look within. Within is the fountain of good, and it will ever bubble up, if thou wilt ever dig."
-Marcus Aurelius

"Running teaches us to keep moving forward, one step at a time, especially in the most painful moments."
-runwicki.org

"The freedom to be yourself is a gift only you can give yourself. But once you do, no one can take it away."
-Doe Zantamata

"A journey of a thousand miles begins with a single step."
-Lau-Tzu

"One of the happiest moments ever is when you find the courage to let go of what you can't change."
-Anonymous

"Occasionally, weep deeply over the life you hoped would be. Grieve the losses, then wash your face. Trust God. And embrace the life you have."
-John Piper

"Owning our story can be hard but not nearly as difficult as spending our lives running from it."
-Brené Brown

"I WILL BEAT HER. I will train harder. I will eat cleaner. I know her weakness. I know her strengths. I've lost to her before, but not this time. She is going down. I have the advantage because I know her well. She is the Old Me."
-Bonnie Pfiester

"If you live for people's acceptance, you will die from their rejection."
-Lecrae

"Authenticity is a collection of choices that we have to make every day. It's about the choice to show up and be real. The choice to be honest. The choice to let our true selves be seen."
-Brené Brown

"Nothing ever goes away until it teaches us what we need to know."
-Pema Chodron

"Faith is taking one step even when you don't see the whole staircase."
-Rev. Dr. Martin Luther King, Jr.

"Recovery is the bridge between who you were and who you choose to be."
-Anonymous

"There are two primary choices in life: to accept conditions as they exist, or accept the responsibility for changing them."
-Denis Waitle

"To love oneself is the beginning of a lifelong romance."
-Oscar Wilde

"I didn't find out who I was, until I found out who I wasn't."
-Paul Carrick Brunson

ACKNOWLEDGEMENTS

*H*ow do you begin to acknowledge all of the parts and people by which you are able to create a story that describes your journey? I will humbly attempt to do so, but if I leave anyone out, please blame it on my mind, not my heart.

I first have to thank my ex-husband and children for allowing me to share my authentic journey with the world. In doing so, our story will help other families do the work and have the freedom to live their truth wherever it leads. Kevin, you were my knight in shining armor and I thank you for the journey that we had. Though we are not a couple any longer, I will always love you, support you, and will continue to be a part of Team Booker. I am grateful for your courage to do the work and be better for yourself and for our kids. Together, we created three amazing souls that challenge us each day to be our very best. Thank you for allowing me to share our story and for showing the world it is possible to separate with grace. To Amber, my oldest, it was you who turned the mirror on me. You challenged me to live what I was trying to teach you, and I will forever be grateful to you for pushing me to be and live my truth. Jordan, my only son, your courage inspired me to be brave.

Because of that, I was able to accomplish things I never thought possible. You always encourage me to follow my dreams and you inspire me with your tenacity to follow your own. Kendall, my youngest and suga muffin, you are my light. Your quiet yet powerful nature continues to keep me grounded in what is most important in life. Your drive to be and do your best is truly remarkable, and I can't wait to see where it takes you!

To my core support network, Edye (mommy), Leah, Kim, Norma, Eric, Clean, Heather, Nicole, Teresa, and Yolanda: You were there through every leg of this journey, even when our own relationships were challenged, your love and support were always present.

Mommy, thank you for being brave, challenging the status quo, for being a trendsetter, and for not following all the rules. The world may not have been ready for you, but you raised two girls that can take off where you started. You may not have accomplished all that your heart desired, but you have left a legacy of strength and power that will live on for generations to come...you are my hero and inspiration!

Leah, my big sister, protector, my ride or die, my belly laughs till you cry, my biggest supporter, my honest critic, and my best friend. You have loved me through my biggest mistakes and sit in the first row of every accomplishment. You have always had my back and because of your undying support I am able to fly on my own.

Kim, your wisdom and advice were a sounding board for me during my most confusing times. Your nonjudgmental way of seeing and hearing me helped me gain the clarity needed to make some crucial decisions on my journey. Norma, your quiet, but powerful presence has always been there, and you always provided a space of peace to just be. Eric, you're my little brother and so much more. Your eagerness to want to hear my story in all its imperfection and not judge my choices, has meant more to me than you could ever know. Clean, your love is undying and no matter what I share or do, you are my ride or die. I love how you love me!

Heather, you know it all. The good, the bad, the ugly, the secrets, and you love me despite it all. You connected with my soul and stayed there ever since. Nicole, you too are my soul sister, and you have walked with me through every leg of this journey with your quiet, safe, and insightful spirit. I am forever grateful for you! Teresa, we have been on a similar journey, providing a nonjudgment zone and a refuge to just talk it all out as long as necessary. You are truly a gift to me. Yolanda, my oldest friend, who is now family. We are sisters who have grown into ourselves and continue to push each other to be better. We are and forever will be.

My coaches and mentors, Ken Williams and Valorie Burton— Ken, you were my first coach and you challenged me to stretch myself in all areas of my life. Even to the point of challenging me to meet Valorie Burton. Your coaching pushed me to be more than I thought I could be and now my thinking continues to BE BIG. Being a life coach and writing my first book evolved from a thought, to an action, and is now a reality, and it began with enrolling in The Capp Institute. I not only met Valorie, but she became my mentor and is now a friend. Valorie, thank you for your friendship, your guidance in the initial chapters of this book, and for the continued collaboration that comes from people who genuinely love what they do and want to do and be more. You are an unexpected gift on this journey and I am grateful for you. To Sylvia High and the Aiming High Family, your transformational coaching changed our lives, and helped my family heal. We are forever grateful!

To my publisher, Mynd Matters, and specifically the Chief Consultant Renita Bryant, from the moment I met you at the *I Am Woman Conference*, I saw that you connected with my vision and passion. Thank you for guiding me through the publishing process and helping me create a purposeful work that will assist in transforming lives. You are a gifted publisher and I look forward to publishing many more books together.

Thank you to my photographer Kelley Raye. I hate photoshoots, but because of your easy personality and great talent were able to capture the essence of who I am. Thank you to my business strategist and web designer, Franka Baly, you are simply the best at what you do, and I thank you for helping me clarify my purpose, vision, and mission and bringing it alive through my website!

There are so many more people that have helped make this book a reality. I thank every subscriber on my website, every conversation big or small, all of my social media followers, all of my clients, and all of the people that have touched or inspired me along the way. Keep living your truth, keep wanting to be better each day, and all your dreams can become a reality.

Keep getting off the porch every day!

To work with Alicia or to learn more:
info@gettingofftheporch.com and
www.gettingofftheporch.com